Integral Astrology

Understanding the Ancient Discipline
in the Contemporary World

By Armand Diaz, Ph.D.

Table of Contents

LIST OF FIGURES

PREFACE

This book presents astrology in light of some of the best of contemporary thinking, approaches that are creating a new paradigm for how we see our selves and the cosmos. The materialistic worldview that dominated Western culture for hundreds of years is beginning to give way, and a new, dynamic, and intelligent multiverse is replacing the cold, mechanical machine that we had come to believe in.

While so much of our thinking is geared towards specialization and particularization, *integral theory* seeks to harmonize disparate fields and bodies of knowledge by recognizing the value in each, and their relationships to each other. *Integral,* which means "whole," implies a view that accounts for different approaches to knowledge and synthesizes them into a whole that is greater than the sum of the parts.

Given that astrology is thousands of years old and currently flowering as perhaps never before, and that integral theory is cutting edge and extraordinarily broad in its transdisciplinary approach, one could reasonably expect a tome running to thousands of pages. Yet I was determined to write a slender volume that is accessible to anyone who is interested, because I think the general ideas presented here are important. I have supplemented the basic text with notes that are not necessary for getting the basic ideas, but are required reading for anyone who wants to fully understand the points that I make, as well as anyone who wants to criticize, complain, or otherwise kvetch.

My intention is to help astrologers gain a better understanding of what and where astrology is, how it got here, where it is going, and where we can take it. I want to provide an integral model for astrology, one that takes into account both diverse astrological approaches and a variety of nonastrological factors. Astrologers are great at doing astrology, but we have to learn to talk to other disciplines, too. In order to make the most of our efforts, we also need to know *who* to talk to.

The starting point for this project is the recognition that our understanding of the world is in the midst of a significant paradigm shift. For a couple of hundred years, a materialist paradigm has reigned in Western culture, peaking in influence in the middle of the 20th century. The materialist view gives absolute importance to matter—physical reality is the *real* reality, and the realms of thought, feeling, soul, and spirit are considered secondary, illusory, and perhaps even nonexistent. During the height of the materialist era other viewpoints essentially went underground, and although they were not necessarily officially suppressed, their influence was minimized by most of our culture.

Then, in the 1960s—what I am going to call the *New Paradigm* began to emerge. Many New Paradigm theorists were encouraged by the advances in physics that had been ongoing since the early part of the century. Humanistic and transpersonal psychologies, chaos and complexity theories, and other disciplines challenged the prevailing materialistic conceptions within the sciences; hence they challenged the entire materialistic worldview. As these fields gained momentum, it was as though isolated streams of thought that had been trickling along separately began to converge into a river.

At the same time, astrology also began to flower. In both astrology and New Paradigm disciplines, what was beyond the fringe began to work its way inwards, towards mainstream culture. Significantly, the New Paradigm and astrology appear to have followed a parallel course, but have done so while maintaining considerable distance from each other. As many New Paradigm disciplines gain wider acceptance, astrology is in danger of being left out.

That's not to say that astrology isn't popular; it clearly is. But it is not popular among the very people who are clearing the way for the acceptance of astrology and other challenges to the materialist view. Consider how rare it is to see even the most prominent astrologers speaking at a meeting on transpersonal psychology, consciousness studies, or global change, and you will see what I mean.

When astrology has been brought into the New Paradigm community, it has been by those who are not astrologers. For example, Stanislav Grof, a psychiatrist, transpersonal psychologist, and psychedelic researcher, has found that astrological transits are useful in predicting the timing and quality of breakthroughs in experiential psychotherapy, and he has related the energies of the four outer planets to the birth process. It is encouraging that someone of Grof's stature would recognize value in astrology; his endorsement of astrology could be seen as an invitation to join the larger community. But we not only want astrology to find its way into the larger New Paradigm, but to *astrologers* as well. Otherwise, astrology will be reinterpreted from the perspective of other disciplines, trimmed and cut to fit the needs of those fields, rather than standing on its own.

Some of that will probably be necessary, in any case. But I think astrologers would have to agree that it would be better if we have a hand in the process rather than leaving it entirely to others. The value others see in astrology is a prerequisite for its acceptance, but it should not be the sole determinant of what astrology is and how it is perceived.

With this book, I am suggesting to astrologers a way to think about astrology that I believe will serve us well. I have no illusions that it represents a complete summary of the direction astrology should take, nor that it is the only possible approach. But we must start somewhere, and we should start soon. This moment in history is ripe with the potential to create a worldview that incorporates and includes astrology, and we should be ready.

INTRODUCTION:
THE BEGINNINGS OF
A MORE INCLUSIVE ASTROLOGY

Several years ago, I attended a lecture on synchronicity given by a well-known physicist, who was promoting his book on the topic. He spoke about the connection between physical and meaningful events, and about how modern physics had apparently discovered their common origin in the fields below the world of subatomic particles. During the question-and-answer portion of the talk, an audience member asked what the physicist thought of Carl Jung's experiments with astrology. It was Jung who coined the term *synchronicity* to describe an acausal connection between events, and I knew well that astrological experiments had figured prominently in his work on the subject.

The physicist looked a bit uncomfortable, and hesitated a moment before answering.

"I think that was unfortunate," he finally said.

I was amazed. Here we were, a room full of people listening to tales about meaningful coincidences and the connections between the physical and symbolic worlds, and yet *even here* astrology—one of the foundational components of the whole notion of synchronicity—was being dismissed as "unfortunate."

Perhaps *amazed* is too strong a word. After all, there was no mention of astrology in the physicist's book on synchronicity. And although physicists, systems theorists, and many other New Paradigm[1] scientists have become very excited in recent decades about various psychic phenomena, very few have been inclined to give astrology much credence.

Although these thinkers have come to see matter and mind as equal partners in the ongoing creation of the universe, most have come to this conclusion after initially working from a materialist perspective; if you read between the lines you'll see that matter usually comes out a smidgeon *more equal* than mind. Talking about the common origin of mind and matter in a quantum field is very different from assuming that the two maintain their relationship at all levels of existence, including that of everyday reality.

I also understand that astrology has had quite a task of trying to explain itself in the modern, postmodern, and integral worlds. Astrologers have been busy trying to dispel myths and inaccuracies about their discipline, while at the same time struggling to create a kind of astrology that is acceptable to the contemporary person; given the inherent skepticism of so many people, that is a heavy challenge. It doesn't help that our calling card to the world is the tabloid sun-sign column, and that quality astrology (even of the sun-sign variety) requires learning a complex language.

Attempts to relate to the world via the scientific method have been unsuccessful, in part because astrology will not be taken seriously by the scientific community regardless of any evidence, but also because the symbolic nature of astrology does not lend itself easily to scientific investigation. In fact, much of science is caught within the materialist paradigm, and explaining astrology and making it acceptable to those with a strictly materialistic outlook is not only impossible, it is the wrong place to focus our efforts. As I said in the preface, we would be better off talking to those scientists (and others) who are already moving beyond the materialist view, although my example of the physicist shows how even that can be an uphill road.

Convincing people that there is validity to astrology is a tough business, and not one that interests me. I would prefer to offer astrologers and those interested in astrology a perspective from which to think about this ancient system in the contemporary world. To do this, we'll have to explore what's been going on in the world beyond astrology, and see what does and does not match up with the astrological view. A major focus will be on *evolution*—not on the evolution of species, but rather on the *evolution of consciousness*. We will also look at the influence of culture and a number of other factors as they relate to astrology.

As recently as the 1980s, it appeared that the field of astrology might follow a typical modern course of development. The foundation of modern thinking is *progress*, a faith that the future will be better, and that the tools to create it are already in our possession. We would survey the past and apply our powers of reason and our contemporary understanding to select what truly works, separating the good astrological wheat from the chaff to construct a single system. Just as modern medicine had liberated itself from the superstitions of folk beliefs and witch doctors, so astrology would be forged into a modern discipline, liberated from the limitations of the past.

Nothing of the sort has happened! In fact, the analogy with medicine turns out to be quite accurate. In the past few decades Western medicine has been challenged in its hegemony over our health, and today a growing field of alternative medicine—which includes mind-body medicine, energy healing, Ayurvedic medicine, Chinese medicine and acupuncture, shamanic healing, and *curanderismo,* as well as many other approaches to wellness—is competing with, and in some cases supplanting, allopathic medicine. In a similar way, astrology did not become the monolithic entity we supposed it would, and in recent years the number of approaches to astrology has multiplied, not diminished. For example, *Project Hindsight* not only informed modern astrologers what techniques their predecessors had used, it actually produced medieval astrologers in the 21st century.

Rafael Nasser, in his book *Under One Sky*, did an extraordinary job of presenting different astrological perspectives and of exploring the underlying similarities and differences among them. His book is a very useful step towards creating an integral astrology. In fact, I believe that Nasser came very close to what I present in this book (and he did so years earlier). The most significant difference is that I explicitly use integral theory to frame the same ideas Nasser presented in 2004. The reader is strongly recommended to *Under One Sky* for many reasons, but especially because it provides first-person presentations of the perspectives of the astrological schools I talk about in the third person.

There have been a number of attempts in the last decade or so to relate astrology to other streams of thought. Many astrologers, including Steven Forrest and Jeffrey Wolf Green, Erin Sullivan, Maurice Fernandez, and Eric Meyers,[2] have recognized the concept of evolution as it relates to consciousness and explicitly incorporated into astrological thinking.

A major theme of this book is the relationship between astrology and current thinking about the evolution of consciousness, cultural influences, and certain New Paradigm ideas. It will show the practicing astrologer, the interested student, and perhaps even a few skeptical physicists, how we can think about astrology as a part of the emerging integral worldview.

We will start off not with astrology, but with a sampling of ways to think about the evolution of consciousness. There are many comprehensive theoretical works on this topic, to which the reader is strongly recommended. For our purposes, we will look at several developmental systems, including the chakras, the integral yoga of Sri Aurobindo, Western systems such as Kabbalah, and the more recent work of *Spiral Dynamics* by Don Beck and Christopher Cowan.

The cornerstone of this book is the notion that these and other developmental systems provide the *vertical* framework of evolution (which describes how consciousness moves upwards in a series of stages), whereas astrology describes the *horizontal* landscape that one encounters at each of those stages. Astrology describes universal conditions that can and do occur at any and all evolutionary levels, yet it says little about the structure of the developmental ladder itself: it only describes the timing and kind of stresses that are encountered. Whether these stresses will lead to evolutionary development for any individual is a question astrology cannot answer.[3]

The true value of astrology can only really be understood when it is given its proper place in the scheme of things. Overextending our reach to make astrology into a *theory of everything* is bound to fail. By correctly identifying the unique contributions that astrology can make to the process of understanding human beings, we will be able to take our seat at the table with the best of contemporary thought.

Anyone reasonably well read in astrology or integral theory will recognize that there are very few—if any—original ideas in this book. What I have done is to cross-reference the two approaches. The more important ideas have already been recognized, often long ago, by at least a few astrologers. Dane Rudhyar wrote as far back as the 1930s on the key points. However, astrologers who were writing even a decade ago did so without the full benefit of contemporary integral theory; as a result their work is sometimes less precise or less fully developed than it might have been. Integral theory is constantly evolving, and really only reached its most recent mature form in the late 1990s.

In addition, the world has changed, and continues to change, in ways that could not have been anticipated just a few years ago. When Rudhyar or more recent astrologers said that astrological interpretation needs to be viewed in light of culture, they recognized that the particular cultural circumstances of an individual would do much to color in the outline of the horoscope. Yet today we live in a globalized world where the cultural landscape is far more complex than it was even as recently as the last half of the 20th century.

Similarly, although the difference between inner and outer directed astrological traditions has also long been recognized, the kind of thinking that goes into each has developed, matured, and increased in complexity. Neither type of astrology is what it was a hundred years ago, because the way we think about ourselves and the world has changed.

My intention in this book is to develop an integral astrology. A brief introduction to integral theory, therefore, seems appropriate. As I said in the preface, integral theory is a way of harmonizing or synthesizing apparently disparate streams of thought and experience; this runs counter to our tendency towards increased specialization that has dominated the past few hundred years. As the word *integral* implies, the theory seeks to *integrate* various streams of understanding and experience. Integral theory recognizes that the value of any field of knowledge can be understood largely by identifying the *perspective*—the set of assumptions that underlie everything that can be known within a field—from which the knowledge emanates.

Once we know where a system of thought is coming from, it is much easier to see how it relates to other fields. I will apply the integral approach both within astrology and to the relationship of astrology to other fields. Applied to astrology, this will give us a more inclusive view of our discipline that honors our diverse traditions. But exactly what does it mean to harmonize and synthesize different approaches?

Imagine a long train journey over some very barren territory. On the train are a geologist, a psychologist, a professor of literature, an artist, a physician, an attorney, and a rabbi. We must hope that they each have a good book for the journey, or that someone has thought to bring a deck of cards, for once the pleasantries and casual conversation are completed, it is unlikely that these intelligent, educated, and talented people will have much to say to each other. Each is an expert within a particular field of knowledge, but it would probably be fairly laborious for any of them to truly speak meaningfully about what they know in a way the others would appreciate.

In fact, my little story is a bit simplistic, since we at least all know what each of these disciplines is, in general outline. More likely, they will each be specialists within their fields. The geologist might specialize in detecting oil reserves from the quality of surface minerals; the psychologist could be a cognitive-behavioral therapist; the physician, a pediatric nephrologist; the attorney might specialize in international trade law with an expertise in South-East Asian countries, and so on. They would have a very difficult time finding a common ground of interest. Leaving aside the tremendous volume of knowledge each has, there is still a gaping void in the very way each of these people approaches that which is important to them. Could a geologist and a pediatric nephrologist have a meaningful conversation? Could they each contribute anything to the others' understanding, not only of the world in general but to their particular discipline?

Now let's visit a backyard gathering in a suburban American neighborhood. Over cocktails and salsa, friendly talk about the kids' soccer league drifts into political and social issues. Conservatives Bob and Mary quickly jump to one side of the issue, challenging liberals Cathy and Fred. Soon, everyone's voice begins to rise in both pitch and volume, necks get tense, faces redden, and the afternoon seems set to implode. An outsider, perhaps lying in her hammock on the other side of the stockade fence, would recognize that neither side is even hearing the other. Each is running its own monologue, assuming the position of the other more than responding to it. Once again, can either side say anything meaningful and enriching to the other? Could common ground be found without a compromise of that which matters to both sociopolitical viewpoints?

In each of these two scenarios, intelligent and thoughtful people experience communication breakdowns. Whether intellectual specialization or emotional attachment is the culprit, it seems the people involved experience a disconnection because they cannot see each other's perspective. The geologist understands an aspect of the inorganic world, the physician understands the body, the psychologist the mind, the rabbi deals with the soul. The conservatives understand the role of tradition and individual responsibility, the liberals know the value of inclusiveness and the strength of the collective. Each perspective has something to offer, but except among like-minded people and experts, it is likely that there is no one to listen.

What integral theories purport to do is to provide a means for bridging the gaps created by intellectual specialization and emotional attachment. Briefly, the basic strategy of integral theories is to identify the perspective from which each person or idea is coming. Understanding the deep *assumptions* that underlie each body of knowledge turns out to be an extraordinarily helpful way to make a connection with it; this is usually far more productive than endless arguments about surface issues.

For example, rather than attempting to understand all the details of medicine, we can start by noting that medicine in the Western world is chiefly concerned with the functions and pathologies of the physical body, more or less apart from the subjective experiences of the patient. We see that preservation of physical life is considered one of the paramount concerns of Western medicine. Additionally, we can recognize that although much of medicine is based on tradition, the use of the scientific method—specifically in controlled studies—is the desired standard for attaining new medical knowledge. We can also notice that some of the greatest achievements in Western medicine have been in controlling infectious diseases, and that military language—the "war on cancer" or a patient's "battle" with a disease—is frequently used in the medical field. Even by making just these few assumptions explicit, it is possible to have a reasonable working knowledge of many current issues in health care. Note that we do not need to have any specific medical knowledge in order to make some very good guesses about the way a patient may experience a trip to the doctor. By learning something about the perspective of Western medicine, we can speak intelligently about many issues, despite our lack of medical expertise.

In fact, when we look at a field from the outside in, we may actually have a better chance of seeing the assumptions (some of which are never explicitly stated) than people who live their lives within that field. When we are steeped in a discipline, we tend to lose sight of the limiting assumptions that serve as constraints not only of what we know, but what we *can* know. Western physicians still have a very hard time recognizing the role of mind and emotion with respect to the physical body, because modern medicine assumes a materialist perspective in which the physical body is independent of our interior experience.

Integral theorists are not shy about suggesting that they *have* come up with a theory of everything. To tell the truth, some seem to be doing a pretty good job of it, although not everyone who says they offer an integral approach does so with the necessary broadness and depth. The suggested readings at the end of this book will help you to find good, readable sources for integral theory.

As much as any other discipline, astrologers are also constrained by their spoken and unspoken assumptions, and in this book I will be making as many of these as possible explicit. In fact, the chapter on the various types of astrology is really about the assumptions that support and limit some of the many schools of astrology. While knowledge of other disciplines is very valuable, it is in our own field that we can make the most of this understanding.

Most typically, integral theories account for both vertical and horizontal perspectives. *Vertical* perspective, as I mentioned, is about the level of consciousness development. Sometimes, this is expressed as the *level of complexity*, and most vertical schemes recognize increasing complexity at higher levels, although complexity is eventually accompanied by increased *clarity*.

The basic idea starts with matter as the grossest form of existence. Life is a higher order organization of matter: a carbon atom in a sunflower will move towards the sun, a *tropism* that you would not see in a carbon atom within a rock. Animals can move about, generally exhibiting more possible responses to stimuli than plants. Somewhere in the hierarchy of animals, a self-reflective consciousness emerges, and this continues to develop and grow until we reach a transcendent, soul or spirit-based stage. Eventually, we might get to the point of pure consciousness, and then to a state of nondual awareness, where the whole vertical, evolutionary process is seen to be an illusion in itself. I will have more to say about vertical development in the next chapters.

Horizontal describes the perspectives we find at each of the vertical levels. For example, we can talk about interior experience, such as thoughts and feelings, or we can talk about measurements from the exterior, such as heart rate and blood pressure. In addition to interior and exterior, we can also make a horizontal distinction between individual and collective perspectives. How I feel about a particular issue will be conditioned by, and will also have an effect on, the values of my family, society, culture, profession, and so on. Integral theorist Ken Wilber uses the interior/exterior and individual/collective distinctions to make two axes, resulting in his four-quadrant model.

Divisions of four are common among horizontal schemes; this includes Jung's types (the four orientations, which are further divided by introvert/extrovert to make eight types), and of course the four elements of astrology. The commonality of the number four in horizontal divisions would appear to be related to the four cardinal directions, and larger numbers are often multiples of four. The trigrams of the Chinese *I Ching*, for example, are eight in number, reflecting the four directions plus their midpoints (north-west, north-east, etc.). However, the Chinese also use the five-element system, and there are four or five elements in the Indian system, depending on how you count *ether*. The nine types of the enneagram also show that not all horizontal systems are tied to the number four, as do many other systems from other disciplines.[4]

However, not all horizontal systems involve personality types. Although almost anything can be turned into a typology, many horizontal approaches describe aspects not of individuals but of groups, physical objects, processes, and complex systems. Astrologers are likely to show the most interest in typologies, but even within astrology we recognize that more than personality type is involved when we talk about the energy of a sign. In this book, the horizontal factors we are going to be mostly concerned with are the interior/exterior distinction and the role of culture.

Take into account both the level of vertical development and the horizontal orientation, and you begin to have a fairly comprehensive view of a person, thing, or system. This is exactly how we will be approaching the various schools of astrology. Once we know something about their vertical and horizontal positions, we can understand where they will be most useful, and where they will break down. More than that, we can begin to outline principles that apply to all astrologies. Some of those principles will be directly related to the content of astrology, and some will be about the form that astrology can take in the future. I present my ideas (or my selection of others' ideas) in this book, but once you understand the principles, you can jump in and develop your own perspective.

Now that we have introduced the basic ideas that we will be covering in this book, we will present ideas about development that are crucial for understanding integral astrology. This material should provide you with everything you need to know to follow the line of thought I present, although you may want to go to the original sources suggested at the back of this book.

Once we've covered the idea of development in general, we will make brief stops to discuss some ideas about culture and the internal/external distinction. Next we'll address the scientific perspective, followed by a short chapter on how consciousness, karma, fate, and free will fit into the picture. Then we will relate these ideas to the various schools of astrology. As you read through the first seven chapters, recognize that each represents a different perspective, another lens through which we can view astrology.

In Chapter 8 we will explicitly outline the basic tenets of an integral astrology. After that, we will make some hypothetical connections among astrology and other disciplines. Finally, we'll cover how the consulting astrologer can apply these ideas can apply in a practical way.

CHAPTER 1
EVOLUTION, PART 1

The evolution, or development, of consciousness is the primary unknown factor in astrological interpretation. It is a variable that is key to the astrological equation, but one that cannot be discovered without an external reference.

The evolution of consciousness is the aspect of integral theory that gets the most attention in this book, partially because it provides a vertical or spiritual dimension to astrology that is sorely needed, and partially because astrology itself is a horizontal or expansive discipline and so provides a system that works on that dimension. Astrologers *could* learn to use other horizontal systems, and they *should* learn to incorporate cultural factors and to think more clearly about the inner/outer distinction, but they *need* to understand the vertical dimension.

Of course, a student of astrology may not have any model of consciousness development at all, and unless they are familiar with some particular spiritual system, it is very likely that they don't. This book presents models of consciousness evolution that will make the concept more accessible to astrologers, and will show the theoretical and practical implications of these systems for astrology. By exploring models of consciousness development in this chapter and the next, we will see that there are many gradations in the evolutionary process, rather than a simple black and white distinction. Consciousness development thereby becomes something we can relate to, in our lives and in the consulting room.

Many people, if not most, have a vague idea about a highly developed level of consciousness, one that is typified in figures such as Buddha or Christ, or perhaps by more recent Indian saints such as Sri Ramakrishna. However, these figures are usually fairly remote from our everyday experience, leading us to a general notion of higher consciousness to be attained at some point in the distant future (such a state certainly seems quite distant to me!). With a more complete understanding of the process of consciousness evolution, we can get past simplistic models where only two stages are recognized: enlightened and unenlightened. Such a simple distinction will have little practical application or even theoretical interest for most astrologers, since virtually everyone we would encounter in a professional context may be assumed to sit on the unenlightened side of the fence.[1]

In this chapter, we're going to explore a simple but useful system for viewing consciousness; in the following chapter we'll look at a variety of developmental systems. Little of the material is astrological, but we'll be relating the ideas in these chapters to astrology throughout the book. As you'll see, a number of prominent astrologers have undertaken similar projects. Our understanding of evolution itself is constantly evolving, however, and there is much benefit in examining a variety of approaches to development.

In 1905, Alan Leo presented a simple developmental system with three tiers. Basically, he said that some people are not very developed and so are pushed about by astrological conditions, some people are very well developed and are essentially above influence, and most people are somewhere in between. For Leo, it was a matter of developing *the will*, which is generally considered to be only one aspect of the overall self-system. However, the real issue with his formulation is that the broad middle tier is not specific enough to be of real use, especially because that is where we are going to find many clients and astrologers. Astrologers such as Rudhyar, Arroyo, and Forrest have also made it clear that how an astrological symbol manifests and the degree of free will a person has are largely dependent on the level of awareness. However, a more elaborate understanding of what is meant by *level of awareness* would help astrologers to not only recognize and appreciate the general idea, but also to incorporate it into practice.

In his book, *Astrology, Karma, and Transformation*, Stephen Arroyo discussed the development of consciousness and how different levels of awareness may affect how a person lives out his or her birth chart. He also talked about the potential for moving upwards towards higher levels of consciousness. Arroyo, building on the work of Dane Rudhyar, thus recognized the importance of development as the missing third dimension of the astrological chart. However, Arroyo did not offer an in-depth, systematic way to approach the development of consciousness; that is what this chapter and the next aim to provide.

Rudhyar *did* describe a system of consciousness evolution, in *The Astrology of Personality*, in which he presented an anthropological approach. Like Spiral Dynamics, which we will discuss in the next chapter (and frequently thereafter), Rudhyar emphasized individual development within a cultural matrix. In this view, not only do individuals evolve, entire cultures and even our collective consciousness as a species (and perhaps beyond) are in a process of evolution. This approach is complementary to those that focus more on individual growth and development, such as the chakra system or Kabbalah. One shouldn't think that these approaches are in conflict with each other simply because they have different emphases. Development is a broad topic.

Follow the ideas in this chapter and the next, understanding that they are going to be used throughout this book. I rely especially heavily on the three categories of preconventional, conventional, and postconventional in later chapters, and I like the system of Spiral Dynamics and use it extensively. We're going to start in the middle of the evolutionary story in this chapter, setting up a system for thinking about ego development that will be helpful for consulting astrologers. In the next chapter, we'll pull back and take a broader view of the evolutionary process.

For a long time, development was considered to be something that began at birth and ended when a person became an adult. The peak of physical development was seen to occur sometime in the later teens, whereas intellectual and emotional development were actually viewed as reaching completion earlier. Jean Piaget saw the entry into formal operational thinking (the ability to manipulate concepts like objects) as beginning around age twelve, and Sigmund Freud's well-know scheme of psychosexual development ended around the same time.

Early psychological models of development such as Piaget's and Freud's regarded development as ending sometime early in life; however, it is now understood that the same types of qualitative and quantitative changes may continue to take place throughout life.[2] It is true that some individuals are finished products relatively early on, but it is by no means the case for everyone. Western psychology has been augmented by spiritual traditions from East and West, as well as newer excursions into the psyche by humanistic and transpersonal psychologies. These show potential for growth throughout life and even across lifetimes, creating not only development, but also a true evolution of consciousness.

It is easy enough to see the developmental process at work early in a human life. From infant to toddler to preschooler to school age to puberty to adolescent to adult, the path of development is well known. We can see growth in intellectual and physical abilities, as well as in the emotional and ethical realms. This growth involves not only the addition of new skills, although that of course occurs, but also the development of entirely new perspectives. An eight-year-old not only knows *more* than a three-year-old, he or she knows *differently*, and operates with greater complexity.

Three-year-olds can think and talk, but they can't *think about talking*. For example, they use words, but cannot tell you what a *word* is. However, a five-year-old has developed the ability to think about words as objects, so that we can begin to teach the child to read, a skill that requires a capacity not only to *use* language, but to *think about* language. That ability (called metalinguistics, meaning *above language*) is at a higher, more complex level than simply using words to talk, and so represents cognitive *development*.

We can see that this development always involves taking more inclusive and more complex perspectives. Starting out as infants, we see the world only from our own perspective, from wherever we are at the moment. Then we begin to develop the capacity to reference other *times*, so that immediate gratification becomes less and less necessary. If we can remember the past and imagine the future, we might be able to wait, to plan, and to avoid unpleasant events.

We also begin to develop the ability to see other peoples' perspectives. If you ask a three-year-old where she left her toy, she may respond, "on the floor." She probably won't say something like, "on the floor at my grandmother's house, when I was there yesterday," not because she doesn't know all of those words, but because three-year-olds cannot usually distinguish what *they* know from what *other people* know. If the three-year-old can picture where the toy is at her grandmother's she will assume you can, too. She cannot take your perspective; she cannot know what you do and do not know. Again, by about five the child will be able to provide you with information that indicates some knowledge of your perspective and what is important to you, such as, "I left it at my grandmother's house."

This ability to see from different perspectives informs every area of life. For example, in the area of moral or ethical development, the young child will be concerned only for themselves and their own wellbeing. What's right is what keeps them out of trouble. Later, there is identification with the rules of society, and what is right is what those rules say. Later still—and not for everyone—abstract principles begin to take over, and concepts such as fairness and equality define what is right. Eventually, rules may be replaced entirely by complex reasoning, for example in the guiding principle that an action is acceptable as long as no other person is harmed, or in Kant's categorical imperative ("can I will that everyone in this situation will always act as I am thinking of acting?").

Higher developmental perspectives truly do become more inclusive, because the earlier way of seeing things is still available to us: my ability to see your perspective doesn't impede my ability to see my own, it *relativizes* it. I'm still capable of seeing the world from my own perspective, but I can also appreciate that there are other ways of seeing, and this capacity changes who I am at a fundamental level. There used to be only *me*, now there is *me + you*; that knowledge creates an understanding that is larger than either perspective by itself. It is a higher level of development.

The progression from taking only one perspective (me) to being able to take another's perspective (you) or a group's (us) to a universal viewpoint (everyone) is seen in all spheres of life. Emotionally, I start out caring about *me*, then I care about *us*, then perhaps one day I will care about *everyone*. The general pattern that we see is what Lawrence Kohlberg described as moving from *preconventional* (it's all about me) to *conventional* (it's all about the group and its rules) to *postconventional* (the most inclusive and abstract perspectives). While each of these three levels can be divided into sublevels, the basic division into three tiers is important enough that we should spend some time exploring each of them individually. They make a handy framework understanding more elaborate developmental models, and they will be very useful as we explore the interaction of development and astrology.

Preconventional Levels

When we talk about a three-year-old, the meaning of the *preconventional* level seems obvious enough: prior to the rules of society. Most people move beyond the preconventional stage fairly early in life—some time during the early school years—in terms of basic cognitive and linguistic development. This wasn't always the case, however. Preconventional was standard operating procedure in human history from our earliest ancestors all the way up through some ancient civilizations (there were traditions, but not explicit rules). It still is the dominant level in some cultures.

Yet even for a contemporary person, emotional, ethical, and other areas of development can lag behind, remaining preconventional. If you think about it, you probably can identify a few people in your life who seem to be stuck in the Terrible Twos well into middle age. The boss who demands that all of his or her employees meet every whim with immediate action comes to mind as an example. You'll sometimes see employers scream at their employees for not anticipating what they wanted done, although they did nothing to communicate their desire; this reflects an inability to take another's perspective.

People who are seriously stuck at preconventional levels, however, tend to be on the outskirts of our society. Because they never learned to follow rules, they comprise a significant percentage of the criminal components of society. Gangs and mobs of all sorts run on a preconventional level, as do many street criminals. In the domain of psychology, people with narcissistic personality disorder and sociopathic disorders are examples of those with preconventional perspectives who may be able to operate at least on the borders of conventional society.

Preconventional adults do not recognize the rules of society; they have difficulty taking any perspective other than their own, and so tend to be unable to exhibit sympathy, empathy, or compassion. We should note, however, that someone who is lagging behind in emotional or ethical development may have relatively strong cognitive abilities—thus making them potentially both functional and/or dangerous.

Preconventional thinking is monochromatic: there is one way to do things, and no variation is possible. It is not a matter of choosing one option, but rather there is simply one option available, and no other choices are even perceived. Safety is the primary goal of any activity; preconventional thinking maintains the same patterns as the default means of preserving safety. For that reason, it is associated with highly ritualistic cultures and with individuals who doggedly resist change. Personal rituals and routines of the "step on a crack, break your mother's back" variety are vestiges of the preconventional view.[3]

Gang leaders, mob bosses, and dictators *do* perceive other options, but these create fear and anxiety rather than liberating opportunity. These preconventional leaders usually have very tough exteriors protecting the not-yet-completely-formed ego and its secret feelings of vulnerability. For them, *options are threats*. There is a single right path out there, and alternatives are seen—literally—as deceptions to lure one away from the one safe alternative.

Although most of us grow beyond the preconventional level relatively early on, development is fueled by two factors: our internal, psychological readiness for change, and external factors that demand we adapt by becoming more inclusive and complex. We do not abandon the healthy aspects of these levels as we continue to develop, although they become *parts* of our world rather than its *totality*, and we continue to utilize them as we evolve.

Conventional Levels

At the conventional levels, people have a strong identification with their group. The sense of self has expanded beyond *me*, and now includes others, to form an *us*. The group itself can vary, and may include one's family, culture, nation, or religion, to name a few possibilities. Whatever the group or groups (for we can belong to more than one), the person at the conventional levels feels their identity closely connected to it. When one has progressed to the conventional level, life itself is so tightly bound to the group that the bond can be stronger than the fear of death itself. Among strongly conventional people, excommunication or banishment is often viewed as worse than death. Strong ties to the group are obviously key components to participation in the military. Of course, not all groups expect or demand extremes of allegiance, but the sense of identity with even a sports team can be very strong.

The conventional levels are closely associated with security and safety, and great faith is placed in The Rules. Because the rules are internalized, breaking them results in guilt.[4] Sometimes the rules are believed to have been given by God, while at other times the rules are recognized as the product of human beings. Whether written in the Bible or the employee handbook, however, the rules take on a transcendent quality, and deviation from them is viewed as a threat that is usually not tolerated regardless of how benign an action is.[5] The more powerful the questionable activity, the more it is regulated and controlled. Sexuality is very powerful, and societies have tended to be merciless in enforcing arbitrary rules about sex out of fear of this primal power. Intellectual activity is also powerful, and conventional perspectives tend to have subtle and not-so-subtle ways of restricting thought, from denigrating dissenting opinions to burning books and controlling Internet access.

Conventional thinking is black and white: there is our way, and there are wrong ways. Unlike preconventional thinking, those who utilize a conventional approach *do* see that there are other options, but those options are *wrong*. It is understood that other people, other cultures, and other religions exist, but they are following the wrong path.

One example of conventional thinking that I encountered many years ago stands out in my mind. A coworker of mine was a young Sikh woman, about to go to India for her arranged marriage. Although our suburban Long Island location was replete with its own conventions, we were all amazed that this woman would consent to marrying someone she had not even met. In my youthful innocence, I asked her if she didn't feel that she had other options, perhaps to meet someone and fall in love before committing to a life with him.

"Oh, yes!" she said forcefully, "Of course I can do whatever I want. I don't have to go to India and marry him. I could stay here, dress like a tramp, and lie down in the gutter with as many men as I want!"

Postconventional Levels

Some people may manage to function reasonably successfully at preconventional levels, and most healthy adults will get as far as the conventional levels. But an ever-increasing number of people are making further strides, into the postconventional levels. At the preconventional levels, a person only identifies with themselves and their own perspective. At the conventional levels, the person identifies with a group and will put the group's importance above their own. At postconventional levels, the group's perspective is transcended in favor of a still more inclusive viewpoint. Instead of accepting the group's ideas and values, people begin to use their own capacities to see past the limitations of the group. Exposure to other cultures and religions are typical catalysts for seeing that the views of one's group are just one possibility among many. Many conventional groups recognize this, and so try to limit exposure (especially of young people) to other cultures. Whatever the proximal cause, someone entering the postconventional levels realizes that choices may be made based on principles such as reason or compassion, rather than on following along with one's peers.

At the preconventional levels, *I care about me*, and that's that. The rest of you suckers can fend for yourself. At the conventional levels, *I care about us*. We're all Americans, or we're all Catholics, or Jews, or Muslims, or for that matter Rotarians, Teamsters, Yankee fans, and so on. If a tsunami in Asia kills a million people, that's too bad, but the conventional person will focus on how many people from his or her own country were affected. The others don't really count. At the postconventional levels, those distinctions are seen as artificial: people are people, with similar needs and feelings regardless of where they were born and other incidentals. A bit higher up in the postconventional worldview, the same consideration might be extended to all animals, and then perhaps to all sentient beings.

Being postconventional means relying on oneself to make judgments, rather than defaulting to the group. However, breaking the rules is not a matter of selfishly doing what one wants without concern for others, but of following a carefully thought (or felt) path that leads to a different conclusion than the group's. Instead of being indifferent to the rules, one *transcends* them.

Early in postconventional development, there is a tendency to rely on principles (justice, democracy) and tools (logic, compassion) to bootstrap one past the conventional viewpoint. Later, a more flexible viewpoint emerges where a variety of principles and tools are available, to be employed as seems appropriate for the situation.

Of course, from the perspective of convention, there is no real difference between preconventional and postconventional behavior: both break the rules, and both are perceived as threats. Each level can only see things from its own perspective or below, but really knows nothing of those above. Someone at a preconventional level has heard of the rules and knows they can get in trouble for breaking them, but has no sense of the intrinsic value of conventional behavior. There is no understanding of the social contract by which people give up their ability to impulsively follow their own will in exchange for relative safety and security. On the other hand, someone at the conventional level will have no real sense that those rules are limitations of their higher as well as their lower motivations. At the conventional level, the rules themselves are considered more important than the goal they were created to serve.

We can take drug use as an example. For the preconventional person, it is simply a matter of "I want to get high and I'm going to get high and I don't care what anyone thinks about it." For the conventional person, using illegal drugs would probably not be an option, as it is wrong *because it breaks the law*. If a conventionally oriented person does use illegal drugs, guilt is a very likely result.

For those at the postconventional levels, the situation is more complex. They are likely to carefully consider the rules and understand their functional effects in both positive and negative manifestations. They may recognize that if drugs were legal there would be many people who would abuse them, and the drugs would be used in inappropriate situations such as while driving. Yet they might also recognize that many societies throughout history have engaged in some manner of intoxication and that there are valuable functions associated with some drugs. They would discern the important qualitative differences between various illegal drugs (something the law often fails to recognize), and they would also understand that the drugs can have varied effects on different people. It might also be part of their reasoning that some degree of risk is involved in every human activity, and if drugs are used with a sense of individual responsibility the only person who runs any risk—if indeed there is a risk—is the user. They might understand that there are psychological and physiological healing potentials in many of the drugs we have made illegal. Political and economic motivations might also be taken into account.

All of that reasoning, however, means very little to those operating from a conventional perspective, and the postconventional person may wind up sharing a jail cell with the preconventional person who was arrested on the same charges. The failure of the conventional levels to understand the difference between preconventional and postconventional perspectives is what Ken Wilber calls the *pre/trans fallacy*. As we go on this book we will see that the pre/trans fallacy is something that is applied to astrology by many people, but it is also an error that astrologers can make when working with their clients.

If preconventional thinking is monochromatic, and conventional is black and white, then postconventional is comprised of shades of grey, and eventually full color. The postconventional approach begins when we begin to see that there are many perspectives that could be valid. The Rules are seen as all-too-human conventions that limit us unnecessarily; we begin to test the world on our own. Using logic and experimentation, we begin to see for ourselves what is true. Initially, at the scientist-businessperson stage, we may continue to assume that there is some truth out there to be discovered, and all we need to do is apply our minds to finding it. Eventually, we can come to a more pluralistic and relativistic stage, where we begin to see that truth depends a great deal on context. If we keep working at it, we notice that these different perspectives all fit together to form a cohesive whole. The postconventional levels don't have any known upper limit; however, most people do not travel very far along the postconventional road, if they exit the conventional levels at all.

Complicating the situation even further, we must recognize that an individual may be more developed in some areas than in others. For example, a person may be postconventional in their career, but conventional in personal relationships. It is not hard to see how the relativistic postconventional approach might work for someone in terms of politics and economics, but when it comes to their own emotional life, they seek conventional security above all else.

Another consideration is that as we transcend each level, we do not leave it behind like a molted shell, but rather carry healthy aspects of it forward. At the postconventional levels, for example, we might benefit from some of the assertiveness of the preconventional levels and the sense of structure and responsibility of the conventional levels. External circumstances can require (or strongly suggest) use of earlier levels: a late night trip through the seedy side of town might call out whatever preconventional toughness we have within us.

The evolution of consciousness has a long history in the world's wisdom traditions. For an astrologer, those traditions might be more easily accessible, so we will take a closer look at a few of them in the next chapter. Keep in mind that this is just a sampling of some well-known systems, and by no means an exhaustive list. We will start in India with a brief description of the koshas and chakras, then move on to Sri Aurobindo, whose work serves as a bridge to some Western perspectives on the evolutionary process.

CHAPTER 2
EVOLUTION, PART II

The Overall Evolutionary Scheme

The preconventional, conventional, and postconventional levels we covered in the previous chapter are in a sense the middle of the evolutionary tale. They refer to general stages of human ego development, but humans are a relatively recent addition to the overall developmental program.

Figure 1 shows a schematic representation of the evolutionary process. Read from bottom to top, we have increasing complexity as time moves forward: matter exists before life comes into the picture, and life represents a more complex organization of matter; mind can only come into being (in this universe) after life has emerged, and represents a higher level of organization (for example, the abilities to move backwards and forwards in time and to hypothesize about possible outcomes); the soul level emerges next, and represents an even higher level of development, one that is not tied to matter; and at the top of the chart is Spirit, which represents both the pinnacle of development and also the totality of the process.

This evolutionary process describes the cosmos as a whole, or at least the history of this planet. First, there was matter, then life; animals began to develop mind, then with self-awareness we began to recognize the soul, and so on. However, that grand process is recapitulated in each of our personal histories, as well. We have to be alive before we can develop our minds, and we need to develop a certain degree of mental ability before we can move to the soul level. In fact, the overall scheme also is valid for each of us at each moment, as long as we are incarnate beings: we must have physical being (matter) to be alive; we have to be alive and biologically sound (have a brain) to develop mental abilities; we have to maintain a degree of mental awareness before we can begin to explore the realm of soul; and we need to be in touch with the soul level before we can gain access to spiritual understanding.

The simplification of the process into five levels is, of course, an extreme condensation of an enormously complex process. For example, when most people talk about evolution, they are referring only to the evolution that has occurred within the broad range of life. The progression from single cell organisms (or simpler) to plants and animals, and then the entire journey from dinosaurs to mammals to hominids, is in itself a wonder of complexity within this band of the total developmental program.

In our Western conception of evolution, we tend to think only of biological change, the creation of new species out of old. In fact, many biologists deny that there is any *value* associated with the progression, and species are only better or less well adapted to their environment, so that humans are no better than, say, roaches, as each of the two species is fairly well adapted to its environment.[1] If a slightly larger context than biology is recognized, then there may be an acknowledgement that in the fifteen billion or so years since the Big Bang, there has been a progression from matter to life to self-reflective consciousness. In this larger view of things, there is an increasing *complexity* in the organization of the universe, although even this increasing complexity is seen as a kind of impersonal condition rather than as a conscious intention. Most sophisticated Western thinkers, in science and elsewhere, are so concerned not to appear to be religious that they cling to a view of evolution as essentially *meaningless*.

Our focus in this book is primarily on the level of *mind*, and for practical purposes most of the emphasis is on the middle range of that level. In fact, most astrologers will be concerned primarily with adult ego development, and the majority of clients will probably fall into the conventional and early postconventional levels (preconventional, conventional, and postconventional approaches are sublevels within the band I'm calling *mind*, although the postconventional reaches up towards the *soul* level).

A broader understanding of the evolutionary process is helpful, even if we only need a small slice of the pyramid in the consulting room. Besides, not all astrologers are concerned exclusively with the concerns of individual clients. For example, weather prediction is the application of astrology to the band of *matter*, and in some senses medical astrology is the application to the band of *life*.

Figure 1. Schematic of the Evolutionary Process

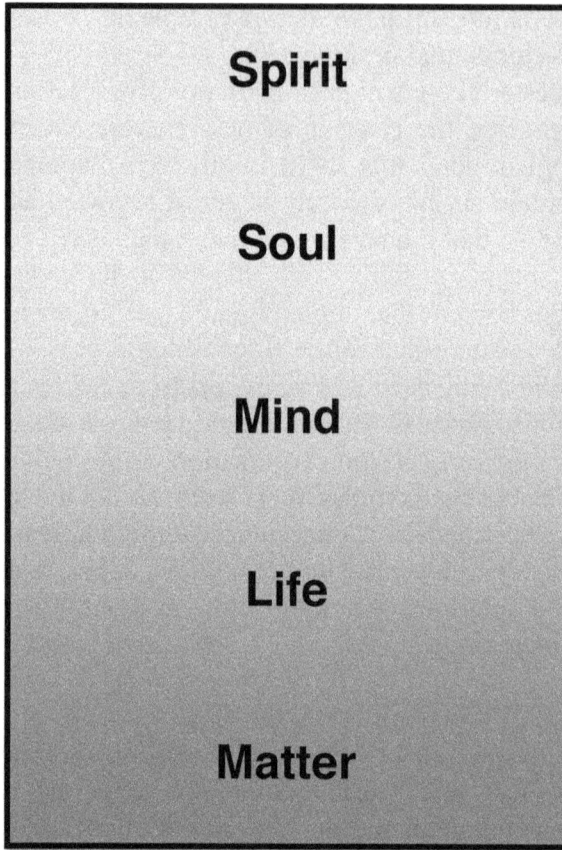

> **Spirit**
>
> **Soul**
>
> **Mind**
>
> **Life**
>
> **Matter**

One other consideration is worth briefly mentioning. As read from bottom to top, the evolutionary scheme proceeds in historical time, from the Big Bang (or some alpha point) onwards. In many philosophical systems over the ages, there has been an appreciation of evolution as a meaningful process. Generally speaking, the idea behind what is sometimes called the *perennial philosophy* is that the original superconscious totality of being hides itself in matter, and then watches as it gradually works its way back from matter through life to mind to greater and greater levels of consciousness until it finally once again reaches the state of superconsciousness, at which point it begins the process all over again. This process of consciousness hiding in matter, or *involution*, followed by its gradual liberation, or *evolution*, occurs in the cosmos as a totality, but also in the individual sparks of consciousness that are within each being, apparently—and only apparently—separate from the original totality of consciousness. Spirit is ever-present, but concealed within soul, which is concealed within mind, which is concealed within life, which is concealed within matter.

With this brief overview, we can start to explore some specific evolutionary systems. Although they acknowledge the entire evolutionary process to an extent, you'll see that most of these systems focus on human development. At the end of the chapter, we'll cover Spiral Dynamics, a system that nicely ties together the themes of this and the previous chapter. Finally, we'll look at astrological developmental systems both ancient and modern.

Koshas

As we've seen, within the process of evolution there are general levels of existence. Although the exact divisions vary and reflect cultural and personal perspectives, there is an overall tendency to locate physical matter at one end of the spectrum and pure consciousness at the other end. The Indian system of the five *koshas*, or sheaths, that surround our pure consciousness, is a simple and elegant approach, and a good beginning for our short survey.

In this view, our true self is undifferentiated consciousness, our personal bit of the totality of consciousness, our atman of Brahman. If we were to realize our true self, we would see that it is The Self, the One, the All, so even our description of it as our personal piece of the totality is only a tool, a limited statement that makes sense only from our limited perspective.

Farthest from the atman is the Annamaya Kosha, the food sheath. This is the physical body, the actual material manifestation of our self. Next is the Pranamaya Kosha, or breath sheath. This sheath is the life force, the principle that animates the physical body.

The Manamaya Kosha is the mind, the mental and emotional sheath. This is the level of the verbal mind: the chatty, restless, clever, and very personal mental processes that are closely tied to emotional reactions.

The Vijnanamaya Kosha, or wisdom sheath is next, and is comprised of intuition and higher mental activity. In our ascent from the lower to the higher levels, we can begin to attain upward-bound wisdom at this level. In involution, as pure being emanates outwards from the True Self, it contracts into ego at this kosha, and it is at the level of the Vijnanamaya Kosha that we form our idea of ourselves as separate beings, our ego.

Surrounding our true self is the Anandamaya Kosha, the bliss sheath. This level is a very subtle layer in which the atman can perceive itself in pure existence. Yogis are careful to warn us that this bliss is not to be confused with the ordinary bliss that the lower sheaths can experience.

The koshas present the evolutionary process in shorthand form. Within this system, we move from matter to life to mind, to higher mind to bliss to pure being in five evolutionary steps, identifying with successively higher levels. It is a good outline to keep in mind as we go through the other systems, since they are all in some ways similar to the levels described by the koshas.

Chakras

Most people have heard of the Indian chakra system. The chakras are described as seven wheels of light that exist within the human body, although on the etheric rather than the physical plane. The wheels are arranged at intervals on a line that extends from the perineum to the crown of the head. Each chakra has an energetic component that is associated with various areas of life, and in this sense all chakras are somewhat active within each of us. For example, the root chakra is located just above the perineum and is associated with basic survival needs, while the sixth chakra is located at the level of the eyes, and is associated with thought. It should be obvious that each of us attends to both of these on a daily basis, meeting our basic needs for food, while also doing intellectual activities like reading this book.

The chakras are arranged in a hierarchy, from bottom to top. If we don't take care of our basic survival first chakra needs, we won't have much opportunity for intellectual activity. Each chakra represents a more inclusive and higher level of function and need than the chakras below it. However, the chakra system also emphasizes the dependence of each level on those below. While adding on a new perspective, the higher chakras must also recognize the importance of more basic needs.

A rough description of the chakras begins with the root chakra, called Muladhara, which as I said is located above the perineum (between the anus and genitals), sometimes described as being at the base of the spine. This chakra is associated with the color red, the lowest end of the spectrum of visible light. When we are operating from this level, we are focused on basic survival needs like food, clothing, and shelter. Our relationships with others are based on a kind of mutual protection, a safety-in-numbers mentality that is seen in gangs and packs of wild dogs.

The second chakra, Svadistana, is located about three inches below the navel. The color is orange, which is a little higher on spectrum of light. This chakra is often associated with sexuality, and indeed that is an important part of this level. The essence of this level, though, is connection with others. Biologically, that does correspond to sexuality, and as animals we need others to procreate. Survival needs shift from the individual to the group or species, although of course sexuality feels very personal and has a strong personal component. At this level, the *Me* can only fully express itself if recognized by *You*.

The third chakra, Manipura, is located at the solar plexus, just below the breastbone, and is associated with the color yellow. Personal power, asserting the will, is the essence of this chakra. As with the second chakra, others are needed to fulfill the functions of this level, although at these levels the other may be seen as an object rather than as a person with their own valid perspective and feelings.

Those limitations recede into the background as we get to the fourth chakra, Anahata. This is the heart chakra, located at the level of the physical heart, although not identical with it. It is at this level that we can truly open to another being's reality, where it is impossible to remain mired in one's own exclusive perspective. Following our way up the color spectrum, this level is associated with the color green. Relationships with others are based on a kind of mutual sympathy, and although that may still be circumscribed by membership in the same group, the feeling is one of giving love without expectations or demands.

The fifth chakra, Vishuddha, is located at the level of the throat, and the related color is blue. This chakra is about creative expression, the opening up of new potentials and the communication of higher meanings.

Between and slightly above the two eyes is the sixth chakra, Ajna, associated with intellect. Although basic mental activity—thinking—is certainly part of the function of this chakra, its higher manifestation is in the kind of intuition or *just knowing* that we would associate with psychic abilities. This chakra is a deep indigo color.

Sahasrara, the crown chakra, is at the top of the head, and is the truly spiritual chakra. It is sometimes described as violet, the color with the highest vibration in the visible spectrum, while at other times it is described as gold, and also as white because it is the sum total of all the colors of the rainbow.

Each of the chakras can be active in an individual at any point in time. If you have an aura photograph taken, or go to a healer who can feel and see your chakra energy, you may learn that your fifth chakra is "open" but that your second chakra is "closed." We always have some of the capabilities of each chakra active all the time, and in that sense, the chakras have a simultaneous quality.

On the other hand, when we consider that there is a chakra that is *most* active, we come across a necessarily developmental aspect of the system. For example, without the security and physical grounding of the first chakra, one cannot really move into the world of the second chakra. The necessity of the first chakra for the function of the second can be as obvious as the fact that when you don't feel well, sex tends not to be on your mind. It's hard to be horny when you're hungry (really hungry, anyway). But we are also attracted to people that have a degree of physical wellbeing and to those who express this through material manifestations (a hot body or a hot car). Thus, we only really get to second chakra relating when we have established first chakra physical being. As another example, the greater function of the fourth chakra—true caring for others—can only exist when one is established in one's self. If the first three chakras, representing physical being, relatedness, and personal power, are not well established, then it is impossible to give love without expecting something in return because there will be an inherent neediness.

So, although each chakra functions in all of us, each of us will operate primarily from one of the chakras. In that development we must go through the chakras in order, so that we must establish ourselves at the first chakra before going on to the second, at the second before moving to the third, and so on. You probably can identify people who are clearly operating from one chakra or another. People for whom romantic love is the be-all and end-all of life are second chakra people. Those concerned with getting ahead and succeeding are operating from the third chakra.

Kundalini yoga utilizes the image of a serpent that rises from the root chakra up to the crown chakra, lighting up each successive chakra as it moves. Sometimes, people who have had the experience of this awakening of kundalini energy report that as one chakra is illuminated, the ones below appear to go cold, which is consistent with the developmental aspect of the chakras—once you get to the fifth chakra, for example, the lower chakras are less attractive and compelling.

Caroline Myss, in her book *Anatomy of the Spirit*, does a wonderful job of discussing the chakras as a developmental system, laying out the challenges and opportunities of each level. She correlates these with Sefirot Tree of Kabbalah and—less convincingly, I think—with the Christian sacraments. There are many good sources for information about the chakras, and this system is certainly one that many New Agers can resonate with easily.

The Integral Yoga of Sri Aurobindo

This Indian spiritual leader's name is not too well known in the West, although his work has been extraordinarily influential. Much of what we think of in terms of the East-West dialogue can be traced to the work of Sri Aurobindo (1872 – 1950), and his influence on pioneering Western thinkers such as Alan Watts and Ken Wilber is hard to overestimate. Interestingly, Aurobindo began life as a political journalist, and really became a spiritual seeker and teacher only when he was imprisoned around his thirtieth birthday—a time astrologers will recognize as the Saturn return.

Aurobindo's system includes not only evolution but also involution, in eight stages. In the descending involutionary process, existence in its pure totality manifests as consciousness force and then bliss, which descends into the supermind, then mind, psyche, life, and finally matter. The evolutionary process is the reverse sequence, from matter up through Existence. Although in its details Aurobindo's system is a unique expression, in outline it is an exemplar of the perennial philosophy.

For Aurobindo, it is the line between *mind*, our everyday mental activity, and *supermind*, a kind of clearly illuminated intuitive seeing, that serves as the demarcation between living from a spiritual, rather than a material, perspective. The system of yoga that Aurobindo devised, integral yoga, involves bringing the supermind down into our lives. In other words, not only do we work our way up the evolutionary ladder, we bring the higher levels down into the world. The higher levels of being thus reorganize and change the motivations of the lower levels. The result is that our material existence begins to more closely reflect the spiritual. Rather than *escaping* the material world for higher planes of existence, we *renovate* it, eventually creating a kind of Heaven on Earth.

In this special twist on the perennial philosophy, Aurobindo is not entirely alone. Mahayana Buddhism, for example, idealizes the *bodhisattva*, a being that holds off on his or her own final liberation until all other beings are saved. The Mahayana ideal differs from the original Theravadan goal of *nirvana*, or the individual's complete liberation and cessation of activity in the material world. Mahayana is more focused on making things better among the suffering creatures at the lower levels of existence. Aurobindo's vision of a spiritually informed material world, however, has few counterparts, and even among those there are few with such optimism and enthusiasm for rapid results. Aurobindo believed that we are on the cusp of the supermind manifesting in the world on a widespread basis.

Whether or not we quickly attain a world informed by the supermind, Aurobindo's version of the involutionary and evolutionary processes is well worth noting. Many systems of the perennial philosophy recognize various levels of existence, arranged from lower to higher in successive approximation to the Godhead. In expecting the arrival of the supermind on the scene, Aurobindo was among the most explicit in stating that the evolutionary process would soon *become conscious of itself.* This concept is something with which contemporary Western evolutionary thinkers like Ken Wilber and Andrew Cohen have recently been working—once we become aware of the process of evolution and understand its workings, we can begin to actually shape the way it occurs. Creation creating itself, informed by spirit.

Interestingly for astrologers, Aurobindo viewed astrology as a valid way of describing the course of people's lives. The astrology he was most familiar with was of course Indian, and in his time it presented as a rather fatalistic system. Aurobindo's assessment of astrology was neither that it should be less fatalistic, nor that it was necessarily accurate for everyone. Rather, he recognized that the fatalistic aspect of astrology worked reasonably well up until the point where an individual developed a spiritual orientation towards life. At that point, all or at least most of the fatalistic aspects of astrology began to dissipate in their influence.[2] This is a very important point, foundational in an integral understanding of astrology.

Western Versions of the Evolutionary Process

The process of evolution from matter to life to mind, and eventually to the One, All-Pervading Consciousness is not exclusively an Eastern idea. Indeed, to the extent that it describes the actual conditions of existence, we wouldn't expect it to be localized to one culture or time—hence the labeling of it as the *perennial* philosophy. It flowers again and again.

Of course, one version of the perennial philosophy can influence others. The system emerges in various forms time and again, but like a perennial plant it often takes a great deal of what has gone before in creating a new formulation. In the West, we often trace the perennial philosophy at least as far back as Plato, although Neoplatonists such as Plotinus were perhaps more clear in their presentation of distinct levels. The Gnostic sects that proliferated around the time of early Christianity were also strongly influenced by and had an influence on this philosophy. Jewish Kabbalah, and to an extent Western alchemy, also relate to the perennial philosophy.

Kabbalah, a system of mysticism developed in the Middle Ages and very popular today, is a particularly good example. The Sephiroth Tree is one of the central images of this system; the material world, Malkhut, is at the lower end of the tree and Ayin, nothingness, is at the other (*nothingness* is another way of formulating *everythingness*, as both are undifferentiated existence). In between are various levels of existence, with one or two types of being at each level. That there can be two manifestations at these intermediate levels is a reflection of the male and female polarities (or yin and yang) that are part of the basic creative process of existence.

As with the Eastern systems, the Western evolutionary systems all posit various levels of existence, and set us the task of working our way up the ladder (or tree) of increasing awareness. With awareness comes freedom, both freedom *from* constraints and limitations, and freedom *to* create and even direct the evolutionary process. As Ken Wilber has pointed out, early versions of the perennial philosophy tended to take the entire process as a given: involution followed by evolution. However, if we think about it, inherent in the idea of evolution is a kind of progress (though the biologists may disagree), and therefore there has to be room for creative variation if evolution is not to be equated with a mechanical cycling of consciousness downward and upward.

Spiral Dynamics

In the 1996, Don Beck and Christopher Cowan published the first edition of *Spiral Dynamics* (SD), a system of value evolution based on the work of Clare Graves. Written in a casual and readable format,[3] they present an extraordinarily clear and concise version of an evolutionary system, drawing correlations among our individual psyches, groups within society, and the historical development of culture.[4] With SD, we will be revisiting the three levels of preconventional, conventional, and postconventional, but adding new sub-levels and filling out the model with much greater detail.

Somewhat like Kabbalah, SD sees development oscillating between two poles, in this case individual and collective values. SD uses a color-coded system: warm colors are tagged to the individualistic *value memes,* and cool colors are associated with the collective value memes. *Memes* in SD terminology can be thought of as clusters of related values that create *worldviews*, and these are arranged in a hierarchy. As with all developmental systems, it is understood that each meme originates in successive order, following upon the previous memes. This order remains constant whether we are talking about an individual's or a collective worldview, for SD deals with the progression of value-based worldviews through history.

Many systems emphasize individual development but assume that the world in general is in a state of decline. In India, for example, there is the cycle of four Yugas, or great ages, each named for a metal. We started out in the gold age, declined to silver, then bronze, and now—you may have guessed it—we are in the Kali Yuga, or Iron Age. Such demoralizing devolutionary thought is also common in the West, and was particularly prominent in the Neptunian 19th century. With this type of thinking, the good old days are behind us, and one does the best one can in the degraded environment in which one finds oneself. Spiritual liberation is the best option, like getting out of a burning house.

A decaying cosmos can certainly provide motivation if one is seeking escape from the material world, but Spiral Dynamics, by contrast, looks at the available historical record (we cannot look back past the beginning of our current universe, at any rate), and notes the increasing awareness and freedom of beings. Of course, there is a great deal of variation among individuals within a culture, and the cultures we see today represent both more and less evolved memes. However, SD notes that the evolutionary potential has never been greater than it is at present.

The first level in SD is the Beige Meme. This level is associated with basic survival needs, and is run pretty much on the basis of instinct. Being a warm meme, it is primarily individualistic, although people at this level may form themselves into groups for mutual protection. Our early ancestors, such as those portrayed at the beginning of the film *2001: A Space Odyssey*, are probably the best referent for this meme, although the Beige meme also describes the level of function of young infants. Among adults, the only examples in contemporary society would be people such as the mentally ill homeless, and those who are seriously limited in their mental functions. Still, we have to remember that we all passed through this stage, if only as babies, and should we find ourselves shipwrecked and alone, we might have to fight hard not to return to this level. The Beige meme is somewhat like a first chakra orientation.

It is much easier to get a handle on the next level, the Purple Meme. This collective value meme is centered upon the group, particularly the connection with ancestors. All kinds of magic and superstitions predominate at the Purple level. Purple is about ritual, sacrifice, and protection through propitiating the ancestors for help. Today, we would associate this meme with tribal cultures, although a good deal of religion remains centered around this meme, along with much of the New Age. Astrology got its start during the era when the Purple Meme was dominant in Western culture, and so it is still closely associated with it. Although astrology has developed and passed through several of the following memes, the Purplish hue sticks to it (and some astrologers do practice from this level).

The Red Meme is the next level up, and following the spiral trajectory it is a warm, individualistic meme. It is, in fact, highly individualistic. Moving away from the collective values of Purple where the individual is inextricably part of the group and cannot imagine his or herself otherwise, at Red the ego begins to form. Historically, this was the age of the pharos, the wildly egocentric kings who stood at the center of their society much the way the ego stands at the center of each individual. At first, only the pharos (or their equivalents in other cultures) had the status of having differentiated egos, but the historic record shows that others soon began emulating royalty, beginning with the aristocracy and ending with the ordinary people.

For example, at first mummification was the privilege only of the king and queen; soon other members of the court were being mummified and entombed; then wealthy merchants; and eventually everyone had at least a chance of a permanent burial place with a preserved body (our embalming processes today continue to reflect this, although in a less dramatic and aesthetically satisfactory way). Elaborate burial rituals, however, are not so much about death as they are about preserving the ego into the next world, for the Red Meme is really all about life. With the ego in full gear, *I*, *me*, and *mine* take precedence over everything else. In general, this meme lives for the moment, and in our society this meme usually views life as short (often a correct assumption for those at Red) and the individual feels his or herself to be in competition with others. All of the trappings of security—from pyramids to handguns—can be traced back to the insecurity of the ego. In the course of individual development, the Red Meme is generally active from the Terrible Twos until the early school years. In some individuals, it represents the high-water mark of their development, and they can often be found in gangs, mobs, or as street criminals. It is associated with pathologies such as narcissistic personality disorder. Constructively, each of us can access the healthy Red Meme within us for the purpose of competitive sports, to assert ourselves, and to protect against physical danger.

The Beige, Purple, and Red memes are preconventional. That changes with a shift back to collective values, at the next value meme, Blue. At Purple, there is really no clear distinction between the individual and the group, and in that sense we could say there really are no individuals. It is as difficult, and pointless, to see an isolated person at this level as it is to talk about a finger without the hand of which it is a component. Mythologist Joseph Campbell described people at this level as "open behind," with the forces of the ancestors, the gods, and the group (or family for a child) informing everything they do. That changes radically at Red, where the personal ego forms and the person can begin to see themselves as separate and distinct from their origins. Red is often viewed as a pathological state, and in our society it can be very difficult for an adult, but it is a necessary step in the independence of the individual.

At Blue, the collective again becomes prominent. However, whereas at Purple the sense of being part of a collective is unquestioned and unconscious, at Blue it is characterized by a degree of conscious participation. Rousseau and other Enlightenment thinkers talked about the *social contract* by which individuals gave up some of their freedoms for the security and benefits of cooperation with others. For Rousseau, and particularly for Freud at a later point, the giving up of freedom of action would always be an irksome, although necessary, compromise. Civilization flourishes at the Blue Meme, but it requires a kind of suppression or sublimation of the energy of Red.

Blue is the meme of convention: conventional morality, conventional values. The individual at this level wants to fit in and conform to society's expectations. The reward for good behavior may be long in coming—delayed even into the next life—but it will arrive for those who are faithful. Historically, this meme reached a kind of peak with the rise of the Catholic Church in the West, although it is also characteristic of many other cultures. Note that the convention to which a person adheres can be very local: their religion, nation, or ethnicity. When you hear talk about family values and such, you are hearing the Blue Meme speaking in our society. This is the meme that wants everyone to "do the right thing," and advocates so strongly for law and order. What to do in any situation is clear, and ethical debates are short and simple. There is a great reverence for authority, and The Word is frequently referenced, whether The Word is written in the Bible, the law, or the employee handbook. Being a collective meme, there is great suspicion of the individualistic memes both below and above, and in fact there is a tendency to confuse the two, blending them into a single category of law-breakers or loose cannons. Within an individual's development, this meme is characteristic of the school years up to around high school, although it is the pinnacle of development for many, if not most, people.

Although Spiral Dynamics is a way to describe both individual and collective development, the process is not seen as being exclusively generated from within the individual or group. Rather, it is in response to changing life conditions that we grow, developing new perspectives when our old ways of viewing the world—our old value systems—no longer serve us. When the individualism of Red reaches a peak and conditions become dangerous, the social contract of Blue emerges and provides relative safety and security.

The individualism of Red reappears in a more sophisticated form in the Orange Meme. This meme only really began to gain traction during the Renaissance, and so it is comparatively new, although there are earlier exemplars of Orange in history. While Red fails to recognize convention and is thus preconventional, Orange transcends convention and is postconventional. The Orange Meme is capable of sophisticated reasoning and abstract thinking; thus those at this level are more inclined to test things out for themselves than to rely on convention. In our individual development, this meme can only arise after we get to the point where the neocortex is fully developed and functioning, at around puberty. Although adolescent questioning of authority has to do with many factors, the biting and sometimes sophomoric arguments of teenagers reflect their sudden realization that they might know better than the rules and mores they have been handed by the older generation.

In contemporary society, Orange can go in two directions. On the one hand, there are what we might call the scientists, using experimentation and logic to solve problems based on evidence. On the other hand, we can identify businesspeople, gaming the system and playing to win. In either case, there is an understanding that the rules are bendable and changeable, not absolute truths, and this allows for not only a simple dichotomy between following and breaking them, but also the possibility of creating new solutions to old problems. Whereas Blue will dutifully learn *what* the rule is, Orange can understand *why* the rule was written and decide on the relative value of both the rule and its purpose. No longer constrained by convention, Orange is the first meme that can actively engage in creating its own world. *Truth* is written with a capital "T" at Blue, but Orange uses a lower-case "t".

Although not necessarily materialistic, there tends to be a great deal of emphasis on rewards within this competitive, individualistic meme. Money, power, and Nobel prizes are all status symbols, recognition of success. Individualistic Red doesn't recognize society; Orange wants to be lauded by it. It is worth pointing out that this meme is dominant in both the world of business and industry and in the academic world, and its materialistic orientation accounts for much of the dismissive attitude towards astrology that we find in our contemporary society.

Moving up a bit and over to the cooler collective side of the spiral, the next value meme is Green. This meme takes the reasoning power of Orange and applies it to community rather than the individual. Also postconventional and freed from traditional values, Green seeks to remake society in a more egalitarian form. Although there were earlier outcroppings, this meme only really began to push its way into the world very recently. The 1960s were the time when this meme began to attract members of the Orange meme (relatively well-educated people, often in universities) who recognized that technological advances and material gains were reaching their peak in value and that a new alternative was needed. Back in the Sixties, the Green Meme fueled the civil rights and women's movements, among others, and was a key part of the music and culture we associate with that decade. The meme has remained active, and while less vocal, it continues to influence society in aspects of New Age spirituality, the Green (eco-environmental) movement, and in the cultural sensitivity training that takes place in workplaces all over the world. Green is an inclusive meme, one that recognizes the value of differing perspectives. A good keyword for Green is *humanistic*.

Whereas Blue embraces conventional society, Green is more refined, and forms affiliations based on shared values and ideals. At Blue, I identify with my group because I am a member of it, while at Green I identify with my group because we share the same values. For the person at Green, being a vegan meditator is more meaningful than being an Italian-American, for example.

Although the combination of creative innovation made possible by being postconventional with the communitarian emphasis on freedom and equality makes for an attractive meme, it is not without its difficulties. For one, this meme is like those previously described in having contempt for the memes below and above it. Green wants fairness and equality for everyone, and maintains a live-and-let-live attitude. However, when it encounters values counter to its own, such as Orange competitiveness or Blue traditionalism, the response tends to be less than compassionate: Greens may see those at Orange as greedy and those at Blue downright stupid. A little further down the spiral, however, Green tends to throw all judgment to the wind and embraces Purple and even Red.

For example, Green correctly identifies the cruelty and unfairness of Blue/Orange colonialism and the exploitation of the Purple/Blue cultures of Africa and Asia by European powers during the colonial era. Yet in denying that there is any basis for a developmental hierarchy at all, Green places all societies and cultures at the same level, with equal seats at the table. That's fine much of the time, but it causes Green to be unable to identify the problems within other cultural systems. Many traditional cultures, for example, are themselves strongly xenophobic, homophobic, and rigidly conventional—the very values Green cannot abide in its own society.

Each of the memes we have covered so far tends to see itself in competition with the others. That is, there is little recognition of the value of the other memes. Even Green, a very sophisticated and holistic meme, has trouble recognizing the value of nearby memes like Blue and Orange, while tending towards a somewhat idealistic vision of Purple, Red, and even Beige. That all the memes, in their healthy forms, have a value for individuals and for society is something that is not part of the thinking of any of these memes. However, Green is not the top of the spiral of evolution, even though it is the last meme that has really pushed its way into society in a big way thus far. These first six memes are called first tier memes in SD, and they are followed by the emerging second tier memes.

First tier memes are all considered to be *survival memes;* these emphasize meeting the needs of physical survival. This changes at the second tier, with the emergence of the *being memes;* these memes emphasize appreciation of being itself. Unlike the first tier memes, those at the second tier are not overly concerned with meeting basic needs and developing security for one or for all. Obviously, this second tier emphasis on being over survival can only occur if those survival needs are being met, although there is some good evidence that once the transition to the second tier is made, even the fear of death begins to lose its power.

The Yellow Meme is, once again, an individualistic meme, one that can manifest when the limits of Green egalitarianism are confronted and a person feels the values of a group—even very good values—are holding back their individual development. The Yellow Meme corresponds very much to psychologist Abraham Maslow's idea of *self-actualization*, the inner drive to realize one's own greatest potential. At Yellow, people have a sense of needing to fulfill their own individual destiny, to make manifest the true self that is within them. There is thus little concern for the values of society, and even abstract ethical principles recede into the background as the person realizes, "I gotta be me." Although for a good many people this stage stands out as a kind of guiding light, comparatively few individuals get to the point of actually operating from the perspective of Yellow.

The Yellow Meme is sometimes called *integral* because there tends to be an appreciation of the entire spiral of development when this level is reached. Although people at Yellow may not spend much time reflecting on such matters (they are probably too busy!), they at least tolerate a wide variety of values. Unlike in the first tier memes, a person at Yellow can appreciate a variety of values at the same time. On any given issue, the person at Yellow will be able to understand that there is value in Blue's quest for security, and that this does not take away from Orange's drive for innovation and change, nor do these two perspectives detract from Green's concern that all are cared for and recognized. Whereas Green wants to create an egalitarian world that conforms to its own values, Yellow tolerates a great range of values that are not necessarily in concert with its own. One of the only times that Yellow gets its dander up is when the values of others are seen as hampering its own development and growth.

Each of the first tier memes represents something of an intellectual innovation on the previous memes. Although the first two postconventional memes, Orange and Green, are so close in intellectual complexity that it has been suggested they are really on the same level, there is some good evidence that Green can encompass Orange logic while seeing things from a more holistic perspective. The move to the second tier at Yellow, however, represents a change towards a new type of development. Cognitive ability has in a sense been maximized, and although it still functions at a high level, further growth and evolution take place with the development of a kind of intuitive knowing. This transition is something like that between the Mental Body (Manamaya Kosha) and the Wisdom Body (Vijnanamaya Kosha). In Sri Aurobindo's terms, Yellow would be a transition stage between Mind and Supermind.

Above Yellow, there is move back to the collective side of the spectrum at Turquoise. This meme is just beginning to come into being, but it is characterized by truly global thinking, an appreciation of the dynamic interaction of systems and systems of systems. At Turquoise, there is a deep intuitive understanding that each part of reality is linked to both the whole and to every other part. Although SD is not a system that is particularly metaphysical, there is recognition that at this level a connection with a transcendent principle begins to emerge (or re-emerge, if we take involution into account). In the kosha system, Turquoise would be associated with being rooted in the Vijnanamaya Kosha.

That Turquoise is characterized by "deep intuitive understanding" is not to be overlooked. Complex thinking and a recognition of the relationship of the parts and the whole is at least possible as soon as Orange is reached, and Green is replete with talk of being holistic. However, mental understanding of a concept is not the same as actually operating from a perspective that is grounded in deep, ongoing experience. That each thing is related to each other thing and to the whole in an irreducible network *is not a concept* at Turquoise, but a description of reality itself.

With regard to the connection to a transcendent reality, the same thing applies. New Age Green can sound very much like Turquoise, but often does so on the basis of very little actual experience of the transcendent, although meditation and psychedelics are two avenues that may offer at least a temporary glimpse of higher realities. In fact, Green interest in metaphysics often confuses Purple spiritism and Turquoise spirituality, seeing them as equivalent if not identical. However, recall that at Purple the individual is "open behind" and thus something like the finger-puppet of the gods. That is not true at Turquoise, where the individual is capable of independent thought and highly creative responses. This difference, as we will see, has very important implications for astrology, along the lines hinted at by Sri Aurobindo.

There are other levels above Turquoise, although SD does not deal with them in great detail, and they are not particularly relevant to our purpose in this book. Each of the higher levels (however many there are) represents a successive approximation to the original spiritual state, the Godhead, the source of creation.

Spiral Dynamics, in its full form, is a very intellectually satisfying system. One reason for this is that accounts for evolution as a dynamic process, an ongoing and open response to changing life conditions. Unlike most of the other systems, it does not posit that the various levels are preexistent conditions that each individual flows through over time. Rather, as the conditions of life change, together with our personal and collective histories, new structures are created in our consciousness and our culture. There *are* seven chakras, but we have *creatively evolved* the stages of Spiral Dynamics, and we will have input into the as-yet undetermined future structures.

Astrological Models of Development

There are several astrological models of development. The ancient idea of planets as *chronocrators* is a kind of developmental system, one that is credited with extending back to the Chaldeans, but which has been updated and changed by various astrologers, including Sepharial.[5] In these systems, the planets represent different ages in the development of an individual, so that the moon represents the first few years of life and its attachment and nourishment needs, Mercury represents the next stage of life and its characteristic acquisition of knowledge, and so on. This model of development is similar in many ways to psychologist Erik Erikson's eight stages of human development (Erikson was a psychoanalyst who somewhat reframed and then extended Freud's stages). It also resonates with the ideas presented in Gail Sheehy's book *Passages*.

The extent to which these systems can be considered developmental models is an important question. They certainly address the early stages of development more or less successfully, although with varying degrees of useful insight. It makes sense that an infant will be focused on lunar issues such as comfort and nourishment, while Jupiterian concerns like the growth of knowledge will be in the background during early life.

Later stages in these models, however, tend to be less about *development* than about the *conditions* that exist at various ages in life. In that sense, we can say that the early stages are developmental or vertical, whereas the descriptions of later stages more closely resemble the horizontal challenges and changes faced by individuals at a given time of life. It is, of course, relatively easy to see development taking place earlier in life, as an infant cries, then coos, then babbles, then says the first few words, and later whole sentences. That a significant qualitative change is taking place is obvious, and that it is a kind of growth is equally apparent. The physical body clearly grows during the early part of life, so that both the physical structure and functions of a person are obviously in parallel phases of development.

By contrast, the changes of later life are less obviously growth-oriented. Particularly when we look from the perspective of biology, we can generally see a decline in the strength and vitality of a person past a certain age. Cognitive and emotional complexity can also reach a plateau relatively early in life; for many people this point is reached even before the peak of physical development. Subsequent experiences and challenges will *change* a person, to be sure, but not necessarily in a way that results in any kind of development, and many people do not really develop very much past a point relatively early in their chronological lives. That helps to explain why the astrological models hold out the possibility that we will gain wisdom and knowledge that will help us accept the changes of later life, and so live more richly, but it is questionable how much they really describe evolution (the same could be said of Erikson and Sheehy's models).

It is estimated that less than half of the population gets to the earliest postconventional stages of development, and that is a recent development. As a consequence, the extension of the astrological models into later life results in a flattening out of the slope of the growth curve past a point relatively early in life, a fair estimation of the progress of most individuals and the population as a whole. We should consider, also, that any developmental model is limited by the evolutionary stage of the theorist. Older astrological models were created at a time when reaching the Blue/conventional/conformist level was quite an achievement (even more recent psychological models such as Freud's and Piaget's tended to top out around this point).

Creating a developmental model isn't easy going. Many developmental theorists today will want to prove themselves in the materialistic environment of the Orange/postconventional scientific community. That will have the unfortunate effect of limiting the model just above the older systems. The more holistic development of the Green/postconventional stage is likely to be seen as too "soft," and the self-actualization of Yellow appears too mystical for those who want to stay grounded in the scientific community.

In fact, there are good reasons why someone working from a scientific/materialist viewpoint cannot see higher stages of development. When we get to the point of self-actualization, the Yellow meme in SD, or above the heart chakra, what Abraham Maslow called *peak experiences* begin to emerge. Additional research has been done on peak experiences in the decades since Maslow first wrote about them. However, for the purposes of this discussion, I would note that peak experiences often involve contacting what Jenny Wade called the *transcendent source of consciousness*[6]. In her theory of consciousness evolution, Wade boldly included research on prenatal and after-death consciousness, as well as data from the world's mystical traditions about the higher levels of consciousness. She distinguished between two types of consciousness: one that is brain-based and develops along with the maturation of the nervous system, and one that is transcendent. Development through at least the first three chakras, and from Beige through Yellow in SD, is development of brain-based consciousness.

The transcendent source is not specifically tied to the physical body until birth. At birth, the transcendent source becomes somehow locked within the brain-based consciousness, perhaps serving as the witness consciousness behind our thoughts and feelings. The transcendent source may emerge occasionally, for example in out-of-body experiences. At death, it is the transcendent source that leaves the body, when the brain-based source of consciousness dies.[7] Importantly for our purposes, some kinds of peak experiences as early as the Yellow (heart chakra) level of development, and virtually all of experience at higher levels, involve contact with the transcendent source. This is a crucial point because it is entirely incompatible with a materialistic conception of development.

It *is* in concert with nonmaterial models of consciousness that are being developed within the New Paradigm sciences. Biologist Rupert Sheldrake, for example, talks about morphic fields, nonmaterial, nonenergetic fields that carry memory and other information. The idea that consciousness is not confined to the physical body—nor created by it—is beginning to gain currency.

I've made this detour into a discussion of peak experiences and the transcendent source of consciousness because it is important to keep in mind as we encounter a more recent and far more comprehensive astrological model of development than the chronocrators, one presented by Bruce Scofield in *The Circuitry of the Self*. Scofield's intention is to show that astrology can serve as a developmental model, not only in parallel to psychological models but superior to them. His model is similar in many ways to that of the older astrological chronocrators, but he uses correlations with modern psychology and more recent astrological thinking. He also relies heavily on the work of Timothy Leary and Robert Anton Wilson, and he has a strongly biological/physical orientation.[8]

Scofield is explicit in his attempt to create a scientifically verifiable model. He is agnostic about nonphysical explanations for astrology, and a result of this orientation is that his theory is challenged at levels above the brain-based source of consciousness; thus we can expect reduced applicability at the upper reaches of evolution, at least as they are described by developmental theorists Wade, Wilber, and the preponderance of mystical traditions.[9] This becomes especially apparent when he considers the outer planets and their *higher octave* cycles. As a result, many of the problems associated with scientific approaches to astrology, discussed in a later chapter, are relevant to Scofield's model.[10]

Scofield has many interesting ideas about development. He relates developmental progress to the cycles of the planets, which act as switches that turn circuits in the nervous system on and off. Early in life, we have what are often called *critical periods* when we are susceptible to the influence of a planet. During that time, we imprint on the energy of that planet, in much the same way that ducklings imprint on the image of the mother duck when they emerge from their shells. After the critical period has ended and we have been imprinted with the planetary function, the influence of the planet is either switched off or at least dimmed down. Scofield refocuses us on the inner planets, using a variety of cycles to explain how their transits can be so significant early in life. The idea that planets have their peak influence on the nervous system at an age that is consistent with their zodiacal cycle is a valuable contribution.

Scofield's model is a true theory, suggesting both a mechanism of how astrology works and describing its effects. That means that the theory is open to a kind of double jeopardy: the correlation of development with the astrological cycles could be right, but the mechanism wrong; or the mechanism could be accurate but the developmental correlations wrong. It would be very challenging to scientifically test even one aspect of the theory, and as Scofield is quick to point out, that isn't likely to happen any time soon. That shouldn't detract from the fact that he has presented a model that *could* be tested. Many astrologers might not accept Scofield's more or less materialistic conception of astrology, but he accomplished what he set out to do. My greatest criticism is that he focused on creating an astrological model that would appeal to materialistic, traditional scientists rather than their New Paradigm peers.[11]

Summary

I have emphasized Spiral Dynamics in this chapter because I think it offers the best avenue of exploring the relationship between astrology and evolutionary development, although as we go forward I will use each of the systems that we have covered within this chapter. Though there are some significant differences among these systems, all assume that there is interplay between a transcendent spiritual reality that exists outside of space and time, and our reality that manifests in stages of development within time. Even Spiral Dynamics makes some mention of a spiritual dimension, demonstrating that a contemporary, evidence-based system will have to acknowledge reports of a transcendent realm from those at the upper reaches of evolution.

A Brief Digression on Astrology and Change

Let's review an important point: there are vertical and horizontal dimensions to any phenomenon: a person (or an area of their life), a group, or even an object. We need to take both into account if we are going to have a fairly complete understanding of anyone or anything.

The vertical dimension is a measure of evolutionary progress, and each successive level brings greater complexity, awareness, and options. The systems covered in the last two chapters are examples of ways of looking at the vertical dimension.

The horizontal dimension describes the unfolding of phenomena at each level, an expansion of potentials into the different areas of existence. The houses of the astrological chart are good examples of a horizontal system—each house is devoted to a particular area of life. We could thus say that someone is operating from a second or third chakra level (vertical dimension) in regard to their second house (horizontal dimension), or that they are conventional (vertical) in their approach to their tenth house (horizontal).

Basically, most categorization systems are horizontal; a distinction between individual and collective, yin and yang, internal and external, good and evil, typologies, and so on, can exist at the various vertical levels. For example, we can see that *good* at the preconventional levels is what is good for me, and evil is what is unpleasant or painful. At the conventional levels, good is what the group agrees is good and evil is anything that challenges that view. At the postconventional levels, we have to use logic and/or compassion to evaluate the outcome of an action and determine its moral value. The point is that the horizontal distinctions remain through multiple vertical levels, although they evolve from level to level.

Figure 2 is a very simple way of showing the vertical and horizontal dimensions in visual form. Within the three levels (which can be anything you like, three chakras, three Spiral Dynamics levels, etc.) the same basic axes are present, dividing each level into four sections. *A* can also be anything you like: one of the four elements, an astrological house, political viewpoint, and so on. *A1* and *A2* are higher, more conscious, levels of *A*.

Change can take many forms. Sometimes, change is about the transitions that occur within a particular vertical level. Things and ideas morph into new forms without really evolving in terms of awareness or complexity. A society can change its political system, or an individual can change jobs, without much in the way of evolutionary growth. At other times, however, change is not just about transitions at a horizontal level, it is about transformation from one level to the next—evolution.

Keeping these two types of change distinct from each other is crucial to our understanding of the dynamics of just about anything, including what is going on in an astrological consultation. The problem gets very tricky, however, because if transitions at a horizontal level create sufficient stress, the result can be vertical transformation. In fact, one of the greatest values of astrology in terms of the evolutionary process is to give us insight into when these stress points will arise and peak.

Most typologies accept that change of type is at least a possibility, but astrology builds that change into its system, so that if a person lives long enough, a modification of the original type is inevitable, by progression, and also as a result of transits. Among typological systems, astrology is unique in its ability to predict the timing of significant changes—changes that may be significant enough to reorganize the person's type (horizontal change) or even change their level of psychospiritual development (vertical change). That's why it is important to distinguish between the changes that can reorganize a given level and vertical development that represents a fundamental change in the capacity of consciousness. Stressful times, challenges, and opportunities all carry the potential for both horizontal change and vertical development, but they also carry the potential for regression, and sometimes nothing very significant at all occurs.

We thus have three dimensions to consider: the vertical evolution of consciousness, the horizontal expanse at each of those levels (such as types), and the temporal changes that occur at each level. It is as if Figure 2 showed a stack of kaleidoscopic images, each level constantly changing, and each level both more refined and complex than the levels below it. In fact, *type* seems a very static term in light of astrology: *dynamic* might be a better choice.

It is important to remember that horizontal features, like sun signs, manifest at every level. That is, there is a first chakra Aries, a second chakra Aries, and so on. Because of that, although a sign may naturally resonate very well with a particular developmental level, we can't really say anything about an individual's evolutionary process based on their sign.

Figure 2. Vertical and Horizontal Dimensions of Phenomena

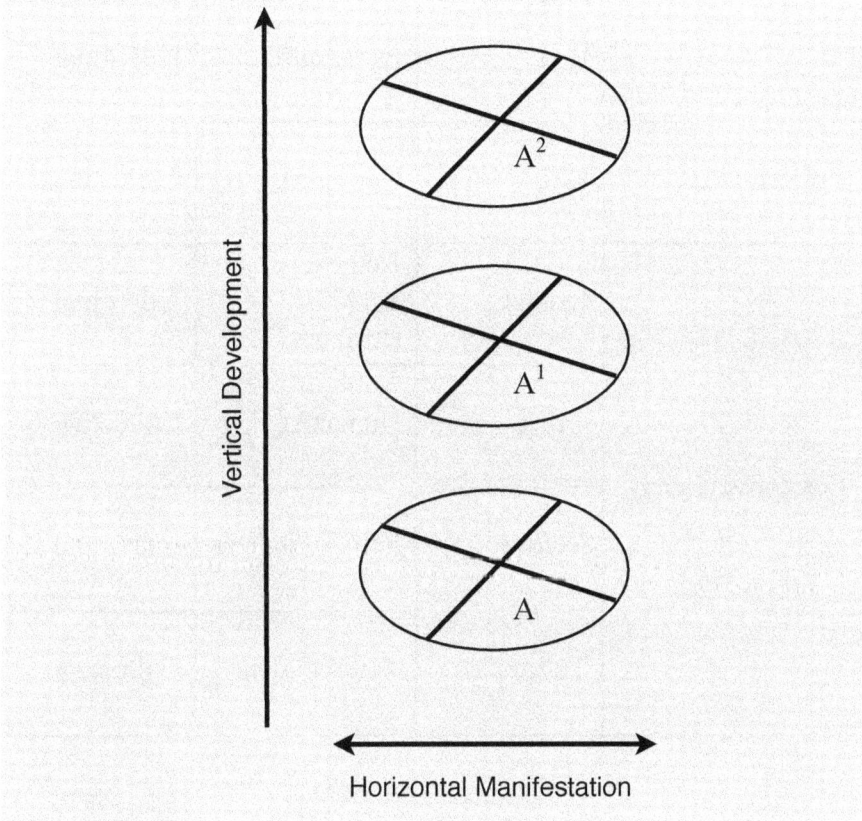

Figure 3. Overview of Developmental Levels

Kohlberg's General Levels	Spiral Dynamics	Keyword (after Wade)	Orientation
	Beige	Survival	Individual
Preconventional	Purple	Tribal	Collective
	Red	Egocentric	Individual
Conventional	Blue	Conformist	Collective
	Orange	Achiever, Scientist, Business	Individual
	Green	Humanist	Collective
Postconventional	Yellow	Self-Actualizer	Individual
	Turquoise	Transcendent	Collective

CHAPTER 3
CULTURE

A culture is set of ideas, beliefs, and practices that frame our view of the world. Culture is learned, transferred from one generation to the next through teaching processes that may be overt, but may also be quite unconscious. For example, in American culture, we overtly teach a set of political and legal values, such as equality before the law, presumption of innocence, one vote for each person, and so on. On the other hand, we also transmit certain values without explicitly stating them. We may not actually teach children that a person's worth is tied to their finances or their career, but in many ways we indicate that such is the case.

We are all embedded in a culture of one sort or another. Cultures can be based on geographic location, religion, and ethnicity, although they can also be based on values and ideals. We can talk about American or Italian culture, speaking about the cultural patterns of nations, or we can talk about the difference between American and European culture. We have no problem recognizing subcultures, so that we identify Italian-Americans, African-Americans, and so on. We also talk about corporate culture to describe what happens within industry. Some cultural labels describe only part of how a person lives, as in Green or New Age culture. Each of us can participate in several cultures.

The effects of culture are more or less inescapable, although the more aware we are the more consciously we can express them. If you live in the United States, you are living within American culture. You might not like many aspects of it and you might feel alienated from what you consider to be mainstream American culture, but in the largest sense American culture contains a plurality of opinions, as do most cultures. And if you live in the United States, you basically have to participate in American cultural patterns. You can't, for example, rely too much on public transport (or bicycles) in most places, as you could in Europe. You can't go into most stores and start haggling over prices, as you could in the Middle East. When you think about it, no matter how you try to avoid it, you are embedded in the culture of the place you live.

You can also identify with a subculture. Perhaps you feel yourself part of an ethnic subculture within the country in which you live. You might also work in a large office, and so participate in corporate culture, or at a university and so be part of the culture of academia. Your interest in astrology might lead you to participate in that culture, too, with its expectations and forms and rituals (conferences, meetings, jokes about astrologers, etc.). In a very real sense, we are our culture(s) because all we know and value is an internalization of what we have learned, although our individual dispositions may help us select among cultures, subcultures, and particular aspects of each.

Culture defines us, and part of the process of definition is limitation. To the extent that we are embedded in a cultural matrix, we have a limited view of the world and limited options for action. Without culture, it is hard to know or communicate anything, but paradoxically, culture also restricts what we can know and communicate. Cultures give us a context for understanding the world, but they tend towards self-perpetuation at the expense of newer, and sometimes more useful, perspectives. It is almost as though cultures are living beings—many of them with fragile egos and strong defenses. Much of the revolutionary energy of the 1960s was aimed at freeing us from some of the more restrictive aspects of culture, although a new culture was created in the process.

Many people have multiple cultures to which they feel they belong (or to which they belong despite their preferences). Importantly, the values, ideals, and behaviors of these cultures and subcultures may not be harmonious with each other. I knew a man who liked to proudly proclaim his membership in three cultures: his profession, the Catholic religion, and the gay community. His profession wasn't an issue, but it is very hard to reconcile a strong identification in religion that is overtly unsympathetic to one's sexual orientation, especially if one has a strong and proud identification with being gay. Such dissonance of cultural values isn't all that unusual, however. Many people fail to recognize it, and most just shrug it off when they do.

Each kind of astrology is also embedded in a culture, and although the particular techniques may transfer out to other cultures, there is going to be a lot that has to revised or jettisoned when making the transition. The greater the gap between the culture of the astrology and that of the astrologer using the system, the more modification will have to take place. The language of the astrology will have to be changed somewhat to reflect the culture it is being used within, but more importantly, the meanings will have to be adjusted. This is obvious enough when an old text talks about how a given aspect will result in "perversions" such as homosexuality.[1]

Even across contemporary cultures, there are going to be differences in interpretation that depend on our cultural point of reference. I have Uranus in partile conjunction with my midheaven, and sure enough I have a rather unique career for a man in Western society. Were I to live in India, however, my work as an astrologer would not be so unusual. In many Asian nations, it is the new generation of office workers who are breaking ground as career revolutionaries—although their jobs would seem very ordinary by American or European standards.

These examples show that we have to be ready to adjust our interpretations to account for culture, and both the culture of the astrologer and the client come into play. We also have to keep in mind that different cultures resonate with different levels of development. Not every individual within a particular culture will be strongly attached to the culture's value meme, but the culture itself will have its thermostat set to a level of development. The degree of attachment and identification with a particular culture tends to reflect the similarity or difference between the individual and the cultural developmental stage. For example, the famous conflict in the United States between the "Red" and "Blue" states could be described as a struggle between conventional and postconventional value systems.

Individuals tend towards identification with a particular set of cultural values, and those are usually in concert with their personal level of development. But individuals are complex, and different areas of life can have different levels of development, as we know. Because the conflicting values can be in different areas of life, living with the conflict can often be done without much trouble. When the values are on the same level, say between two religious viewpoints, there might be more difficulty, although people are very accommodating when it comes to living with dissonance.

There are many systems for understanding culture. As with other things, integral theory suggests that we should look at the assumptions that underlie surface manifestations and so try to understand the culture's perspective.

Once again, Dane Rudhyar was well ahead of his time in recognizing the importance of culture and how it affects astrological interpretation. However, although he saw that astrology would vary among cultures, at the time he was writing he could not have foreseen how very different astrologies would eventually coexist. He also could not have anticipated the extraordinary cultural confluence that occurred in the last half of the 20th century, nor that astrological approaches from across time and space would each be acknowledged (or resurrected) as living astrologies, side by side with each other.

It can become rather complex, but culture and cultural values are key points in understanding where an astrology is coming from, and who it is serving. In the past, an astrologer, his astrology, and his client were most likely all within the same cultural sphere, and the standards of that culture were probably very clear. Today, it is more than possible to be a Jewish Jyotish astrologer in American culture, meeting with a Christian Japanese client who is visiting from his job in Europe.

Culture matters.

Gender Roles

Gender is an aspect of culture that is especially relevant for astrologers. Because astrology extends so far back in time, much of its terminology and a good many of its concepts are from eras when people thought very differently about gender than we do today. Some aspects of the masculine/feminine distinction may be timeless, but many of them are antiquated. Knowing what to keep and what to discard (or at least relativize) is crucial, especially in our contemporary world where gender itself is evolving as fast as our ways of talking about it.

Not long ago, there were no women police officers. Police work is dangerous even to the point of being life-threatening, it involves contact with some very undesirable members of society, and it requires (at least in potential) a great deal of physical effort. Certainly, police work is a man's world, and no place for a lady. Or so the thinking went until a small group of maverick women began to challenge the accepted thinking a few decades ago. It turns out that women *can* do police work as well as men, and today female officers are almost as common as male.

At the same time, though, it is fair to say that the nature of police work has also changed. In a previous era, a cop could whack a guy standing on the street corner and tell him to move along, and that's no longer acceptable (it *happens*, but it's not *acceptable*). Many of the more physical and aggressive aspects of police work have been modified over the years by changes in attitudes and technology. Women entered a changing profession, and then further contributed to that change, so that the career they are so prominent in today is very different from that they were excluded from years ago.

Women have also made significant inroads into the military. Although many report sexual harassment and even rape (and they generally report it outside of the military), women have established themselves in highly aggressive combat roles. As the United States learned in Iraq, they even showed that they could engage in the same kinds of aggressive misbehavior for which male soldiers are known.

By comparison, there are very few women firefighters. Firefighting has always been less associated with the kind of aggression that is typical in police work, and many fire companies today would probably be far more willing to accept women than police departments in years past. But firefighting is extremely demanding physically—most firefighters are big and all are strong. Few women can realistically compete for jobs in this area, showing us that some gender distinctions are not entirely based on internal disposition.

In the corporate world and in academia, women have also made great strides into what was once a man's world. They have shown that they can participate in the competitive, if not outright aggressive, business environment (although their pay is still typically less than men's).

In the 1950s, my mother was the only female mechanical engineer at an aerospace company. At one point, she took a course at local college to learn some mathematical techniques. The professor came in and surveyed the class of about twenty men and one woman. "Excuse me, miss," he said, "but secretaries aren't allowed to take this course." Although she remained in the course and received a decent grade, the professor did everything possible to exclude and belittle her, so offended was he to see a woman engineer. At her job, too, she had a degree of harassment to put up with: parts and plans would go missing, deliveries would never arrive, and of course there were constant comments and remarks from her machismo coworkers. None of that stopped the company from recognizing that a female engineer was a unique commodity, and they didn't mind sending her on assignments where she would meet with customers and government liaisons. Although they valued her as an engineer, they valued her more as a *female* engineer.

Just a generation or so later, the situation is radically different. Across the Western world, women are more likely to complete degrees in higher education than men. Although the concentration of women varies by field, no professor today can look out over a class of engineers, physicians, or other professionals and assume the woman in the class is a secretary.

Because we place such value on outgoing, assertive, competitive professions in our society, we hear less about the reverse process. Relatively few men go into the more caring, supportive professions like nursing. I teach speech pathology students in college and graduate school, and it is unusual to find even a single male among a class of thirty women. Significantly, when they do go into these otherwise female professions, men often achieve high-status positions within them (a similar pattern is apparent in astrology). While they may be a relative rarity in some fields, the men that have gone into professions like nursing have no doubt had an effect on those professions and how they are perceived. As with police work, each of these professions has changed and evolved in many ways over the years.

The point is that we are coming to recognize, albeit slowly as a society, that one's external genitalia and one's internal disposition do not necessarily correlate in predictable ways. Gender identification and gender roles are fluid, and neither is entirely dependent on the physical body. There may be parameters that are set by one's physical form, but these are practical more than temperamental. We are even approaching a point of official recognition of this fact. For example, in New York City, one can declare one's gender on any official city form based on identification rather than physical characteristics, so that a bearded person with a penis can declare that she is female.

The implications of all of this for astrologers should be obvious. Consider that we have a history that talks about male and female signs. The male signs are recognized as outgoing, assertive, and bright, whereas the female signs are seen as inwardly directed, passive, and dark (an interesting coordination with the color scheme of Spiral Dynamics is suggested). Many astrologers recognize the difficulties involved in calling these distinctions male and female, and so they will use more neutral terms like yang and yin. By using more gender-neutral terms, we remove the sense that a Gemini woman or a Virgo man is somehow an oxymoron.[2]

There are more complicated aspects of gender, as well. For example, in traditional astrology, the sun in a woman's chart was seen as representing the men in her life. Therefore, a transit of Saturn to the sun might be expected to have some difficult effect on her husband. That view assumes that the solar functions of life for a woman are lived out through other people, specifically men. It is as though a woman does not really have a sun in her chart, but a placeholder to be filled by someone else. Given what I've said about how gender roles are changing, such a view is unacceptable in the contemporary world. Women always had the *potential* to live out their solar functions themselves, but it is blatantly obvious that they now also have the *opportunity*. However, for a woman with a strong traditional, conventional view of herself (depending on the specific conventions), the sun may in fact stand for the men in her life.

In a complementary way, the moon was seen as representing the women in a man's life. Because the moon is associated with the feminine characteristics of nurturing and the feeling side of life, men caught up in traditional roles had to farm the lunar function out to women and live it vicariously. As we have softened gender roles, this has become less necessary, and men can experience this side of themselves firsthand as well as through others.

Considering the moon gives us pause, though. The masculine and feminine, or yang and yin, *are* different, and they represent polarities within the manifest world. To some extent they are rooted in the physical body, although we are moving towards a time when physical differences are seen as parameters rather than comprehensive determinants of either internal disposition or external behavior. Yet the distinctions we associate with them, such as outgoing and receptive, are important to recognize. In transcending physical gender, we can bring the experience of these polarities to a higher level, but should not negate them entirely.

Gender at the Collective Level

The drive to transcend gender is fueled in large part by the recognition that our limited view of the masculine and the feminine is the cause of a great deal of trouble in the collective as well as within individuals. One version of this is the distinction between matriarchy, culture based in the feminine, and patriarchy, the male-dominated culture that is usually seen as having pervaded the West for several thousand years.

Riane Eisler's popular book, *The Chalice and the Blade*, begins with this distinction, although in recognition that these two cultural styles are not actually associated with physical gender (men aren't necessarily the bad guys), she renames patriarchy *dominator* culture, while matriarchy becomes *partnership* culture (or *gylanic*, a neologism that incorporates both *gyno* and *anthro*).[3] Despite Eisler's assertion that dominator culture is not entirely a male affair, nor partnership entirely feminine in nature, she recognizes that dominator culture necessarily involves a great deal of subjugation of feminine energy. Eisler joins with many others, including Terence McKenna and Andrew Harvey, in calling for (or simply recognizing) the reemergence of the feminine to balance the excesses of patriarchal, dominator culture.

There is a problem inherent in this view, as expressed by Eisler, in that it collapses all of cultural evolution into two camps that seem to reincarnate at different times and in different places. Reading *The Chalice and the Blade*, it is very hard to get a sense of *why* things have gone so terribly wrong for so very long. For example, Eisler paints a rather idealized picture of Minoan Crete as a gylanic partnership culture that was thriving before being supplanted by the invasion of northern tribes that carried a dominator culture. The story of nomadic hunter tribes that invade agrarian civilizations is a familiar one, and in addition to Minoan Crete we can see similar processes in the Indus Valley civilizations, the Mongol invasions, and elsewhere, too. Yet Eisler describes the invading tribes as more or less uncultured thugs; although that may be a valid portrayal, the reader is left wondering why they then prevailed not only in Crete, but also throughout Western civilization and much of the world.

There are two unfortunate consequences of the limitations of this view. The first is that it tends to stir up a sense of collective guilt. We have been unconsciously perpetuating a patriarchal, dominator culture for thousands of years, doing untold harm to each other and our fellow creatures on the planet. The sense of shame for the enslavement and exploitation is immense, despite the fact that many of us have not actively participated in the harm that was done in our name. In fact, it is typically those of us who tend towards partnership value systems that feel the guilt most acutely. In *Spiral Dynamics*, Beck and Cowan point out that this sense of collective guilt is very typical of the humanitarian Green value meme. Although recognition of the problem and efforts to correct it are to be lauded, sinking into a collective self-recrimination is not necessarily the best way to go about making productive changes, particularly because it often throws out the cultural baby with the bath water. Western culture has done some good things, too.

The second problem is that although the basic dominator/partnership dichotomy may be valid, it does not explain the complex patterns of cultural evolution. In short, it reduces cultural evolution to two steps: matriarchy followed by patriarchy. Since the focus on patriarchy is on the negatives (and there are many), we actually wind up with a kind of cultural *devolution*. The good old days of Minoan Crete, Harappa, Mohenjo Daro, and

Machu Pichu are behind us, and we must resurrect them if we are to again become whole, civilized, and perhaps even if we are to survive at all. Yet prepatriarchal cultures had their problems, too. Although the feeling of being part of an organic whole had value, it is unlikely that a fully formed individual in the 21st century would like to participate in the kind of cultural constraints that were part of most early civilizations.

Harkening back to a past golden age and trying to drive contemporary civilization there is highly problematic, if for no other reason than that it actually ignores much of the evolution that has taken place. Were there simply wholesome, integrated, organic partnership cultures and fragmented, hierarchal, artificial dominator cultures, the choice would be easy. But that is not the case, and we have already encountered a much better model for looking at the process, in Spiral Dynamics. Recall that in SD, evolution of both individuals and cultures oscillates between two poles, the warm colors (Beige, Red, Orange, and Yellow) that are focused on the individual and the cool colors (Purple, Blue, Green, and Turquoise) where the focus is more on the collective.

There is an obvious parallel between the warm colors in SD and dominator culture, whereas the cool colors resonate with partnership culture. Spiral Dynamics adds a truly evolutionary perspective, in that both the warm and cool colors are recognized as manifesting at different levels of consciousness: Red is above Beige, Orange is above Red, and so on. More than that, SD posits that development takes place in a sequence that oscillates between the warm and cool colors, thus answering the question of why patriarchal culture seems to be so enduring: the warm colors of the spiral of evolution are a necessary part of the process. Although recognizing that the various value memes can in fact be dominant in a culture (the Middle East is Blue, conformist, and conventional while modern Europe is Orange, postconventional), SD sees that a variety of value memes are operative within any culture at any given point in time. It is a complex process, and the reader is again referred to the original sources, but if it is true that development proceeds in an invariant sequence in both individuals and cultures, then the warm side of the spectrum is not only always going to be with us, it is actually *necessary* for evolution.

If we use Eisler's terminology, we find ourselves assigning positive and negative values to the two sides of the developmental spiral. Warm colors are bad, cool colors are good. I think we would do better to realize, as Beck and Cowan have said, that there are healthy and unhealthy manifestations of the more individualized value memes, and the same is true of the more collectively oriented memes. The warm colored value memes do not create societies that are necessarily patriarchal, patriarchy is a distortion and exaggeration of the warm memes, and the collectively oriented cool memes are not without their problems.

Rather than seeing a simple dichotomy between partnership and dominator societies, or matriarchy and patriarchy, we can then differentiate between the egocentric Red culture of pharaonic Egypt, the Aryan nomads, or the Mongols, and the Orange culture of corporate America. Yes, we can see parallels, as the term *corporate raider* suggests. But we can also see differences. We can also differentiate—and perhaps this is more important—between the Purple tribal cultures of indigenous tribes, where individuality is not fully developed, and the Green, humanitarian social movements. The women's movement, or the civil rights movement, or the green movement, for example, are collectives of fully formed postconventional individuals, not organically related members of a tribe. If we take the view suggested by SD, we do not need to go back to the past to create a healthy, gylanic, partnership culture. Instead, we can evolve towards a higher-order partnership culture than has ever been seen before.

Astrologers Steven Forrest and Jeffrey Wolf Green also emphasized the importance of culture in astrological interpretation, making the distinction between matriarchy and patriarchy in their book, *Measuring the Night*. They saw the patriarchy as having been most influential over the past six thousand years, having supplanted the more organic matriarchal cultures that existed beforehand. In a matriarchal culture, some vestiges of which survive today in indigenous tribes, there is a sense of wholeness and a recognition that everyone and everything contributes to the totality of the culture. By contrast, within a patriarchy there is a hierarchy wherein some elements and some people become more important than others. Patriarchies lead to oppression and alienation.

Like Eisler, Forrest and Green did a good job of showing the damages done by thousands of years of patriarchy, extending into our own cultural habits, but can do little to explain why such a blatantly dysfunctional pattern became the norm. They outlined a process of intimidation and subjugation that helps dominator culture to maintain itself, but can thousands of years of civilization be based entirely on carrying a big stick?

Once again, I thank my fellow astrologers for their patience in considering some very non-astrological material. The points made in this section are relevant to astrology, however. How we view the culture we are in, and how we view the culture of a client, will affect our readings, and it is wise to be as aware as possible of the process that is taking place. The patriarchy/matriarchy distinction also figures prominently in evolutionary astrology, as articulated by Steven Forrest and Jeffrey Wolf Green.

Culture and Values

We already know a lot about culture and values. The memes of Spiral Dynamics are called *value memes*, after all, and they express values that are embraced at different levels of development. The Blue, conventional, meme values tradition and the rules, for example.

But which rules? The rules of conformist China are different from those of conformist America. The traditional values of each culture are very different, as well. What is accepted and encouraged in one culture can be totally unacceptable in another. Monogamy is the traditional value throughout the West, but polygamy is part of some Eastern cultures. Each of these views is normal for those who live within those cultures. A north-Indian polygamist might be very conservative within his culture, as radical as he would be in Europe or America.

It is not just traditional values that vary. Postconventional values will vary, by definition. The scientific, achievement orientation (Orange) can be channeled into research, or it can be directed towards the world of business. Egalitarian Green values can be expressed in the ecological movement or in New Age spirituality, or even in a postconventional approach to a traditional religion (many people are engaged in trying to save at least some aspects of the Big Three Western religions). Down at the lower end of the spiral, the Purple tribal cultures will all have their own customs, as will their Red leaders. The cultural determinants of values vary. A person can be a conventional Republican or Democrat, or a postconventional version of either.

That means that we have to be able to see developmental level and cultural perspective as two different things, although within the individual they will of course be related. Astrologers need to be careful not to prejudge a person based on the specific values they are espousing (these often come up when they are discussing issues relevant to a reading). Rather, it is important to get a sense of why a person is identifying with a particular belief. Often, it is simply enough to ask why a viewpoint is so important to them.

Sexuality

Sexuality is often regarded of as being closely related to gender, and it is, but I have put a little space between the two in this chapter so that we can differentiate clearly between them. Sexuality is a very broad topic, and it does include gender identification as well as sexual orientation (what someone finds sexually attractive), lifestyle (how they incorporate sexuality into their lives, independent of what they find attractive) and cultural attitudes towards sexuality.

Again, much of traditional astrology was formulated at a time when attitudes towards sexuality were highly conformist. Until the 1960s, for example, homosexuality was a crime in Great Britain. Many states in the United States still have similar laws, and they are sometimes enforced. That gay marriage has become such a prominent issue is quite a positive development, but in the resistance to it we can see that sexual mores do not change easily.

Homosexuality has steadily worked its way in from the periphery of society since the start of the gay rights movement in the late 1960s, but it is not the only aspect of sexuality that is put under scrutiny by conventional societies. In fact, virtually all of sexuality is highly regulated in most conventional cultures. Who a person has sex with, when, where, and even what specific acts and in what positions, are regulated by laws, religion, and/or societal mores.

Astrologers will recognize that as the outer planets passed through Libra and Scorpio in the second half of the 20th century, relationship patterns and sexual mores changed a great deal, and Western culture now has a more open and accepting attitude towards a variety of sexual lifestyles. However, once again we cannot assume a client's attitude towards sexual issues. Not all cultures have accepted the changes in sexual ethics, and even within Western culture there is a gradient that we need to recognize (Kansas is different from New York is different from the Netherlands).

As clients may be participating in more than one culture and at more than one developmental level, the picture can get very complex. An orthodox Jewish woman I know felt bound to live a monogamous life with someone from her own religious background, and would not tolerate the idea of marrying outside of her faith despite her attraction to a Christian man. However, she also had several sexual experiences with women, something she casually accepted as typical despite the strong condemnation same-sex relationships received within her religious community. As with so many aspects of culture, the interaction of several distinct and mutually exclusive viewpoints can produce odd combinations of belief and behavior. This woman was conventional and identified with her religion in regard to *marriage*, but postconventional with regard to same-sex relationships. Astrologers need to recognize that this kind process is going on in many areas of life for many clients, and to be aware that clients can be casual about some aspects of sexuality while suffering with others. It is a complex picture and it can be difficult to understand, but it's better than in previous times, when nearly everyone suffered over all aspects of sexuality.

Religion

As someone born in the second half of the 20th century, the idea that religious values would have a major impact on life in the Western world seemed ridiculous to me. The only differences among religions that seemed to matter when I was growing up were on the order of what people ate on their holidays. As far as the underlying belief system was concerned, no one I knew really took it seriously. The scientific-materialist culture had turned many of us into suburbanite atheists or agnostics, if we thought about it at all.

Gradually, however, religion began to reemerge. In the United States, Jesus freaks became born-again Christians, and soon the Religious Right was influencing politics. A great wave of migration distributed people with various religious attitudes all over the globe, so that Muslims are now well-represented in Europe and America, just as Korean Christians have taken their devotion to secular New York. Once again, religion matters.[4]

Religion is a powerful force. On the one hand, it represents an ultimate perspective, the bottom line of existence for its adherents. If God wants you to do something, you had better do it. If God doesn't want you to do something, you should not let him see you doing it. Religion as an ultimate perspective is something that can relativize every other aspect of a person's worldview. As Freud realized, much of the symbolism of religion is tied to the parents ("Our Father who art in heaven") and powerful feelings about the father and mother are often associated with religion.

To a great extent, religion is uncritically accepted. Because it is usually something that is presented very early in life, and because it is presented as the ultimate truth, many people have a hard time transcending their religion, and quite a few have no desire to do so.

Science and religion do not get along very well (in fact, their mutual condemnation of astrology is one of the few points of agreement science and Western religions have, although they attack astrology from different perspectives). For science, religion is superstition, and scientists have persecution by the Church stored in their collective memories. For religion, science is a threat because it seems to offer its own ultimate perspective and so is seen as encroaching on religion's territory. Neither side tends to know much about spirituality.[5]

Astrologers need to be aware of the strong influence religion can have. Religion can be an aspect of a person's worldview that lags behind other areas, often serving as a kind of anchor in the conventional stages of development even when career, relationship, and other areas have gone on to postconventional levels. For many clients who are more firmly rooted in the conventional mores of Western religions, even a visit to an astrologer can require an almost heroic act of personal courage. For clients who come from an Eastern religious background, astrology may not be a challenge to their religious beliefs, but many of the issues for which they consult an astrologer may challenge those beliefs.

Summary

In this chapter we have taken a brief look at a few topics relating to culture that can serve as examples of why culture matters. Many more issues could be discussed, including the interaction of various cultural factors. Even relatively recently, astrologers could make assumptions about a client's cultural background, and although it was recognized that the same astrological factor would manifest differently in different cultures, we now live in a world where even within a single individual there may be an identification with a variety of cultural perspectives. Part of an astrologer's job is to help the client sort out how these cultural beliefs work with their chart, and to eventually get to a place where they have at least a self-consistent view of the world.

CHAPTER 4
INSIDE-OUT—THE THORNY PROBLEM OF INTERIOR AND EXTERIOR

In our discussions of integral theory thus far, I have emphasized the developmental and cultural aspects of the system. The evolution of consciousness is a key part of understanding any phenomenon, since both the observer and the observed will have their own distinct levels of consciousness. Cultural factors necessarily determine how anything is perceived and acted upon. There is, however, another distinction that needs to be considered: one that operates on each evolutionary level.

For our purposes, we can recognize a basic dichotomy in approaches to understanding, between those that are inner-directed or subjective in their emphasis, and those that are outer-directed or objective. Within astrology, this dichotomy is often presented as *psychological* and *event-orient* systems.[1]

The distinction between inner- and outer-directed is a bit like a holographic projection. It appears to be there, but when you try to grab it, it vanishes. It is a useful dichotomy when seen from a distance, but it becomes less helpful as we get closer.

Perhaps the most well known example of the inner/outer distinction is Jung's concepts of introvert and extrovert. In popular use, introverts are usually considered to be shy and withdrawn, whereas extroverts are outgoing and sociable. Jung did say some things that support that way of thinking about these two orientations, but his actual definitions are a bit more complex.

Introverts are people who have an inner standard, and they compare external stimuli to that standard. In other words, they judge the world according to their own viewpoint. Extroverts have the reverse situation, and they judge themselves by external standards. Coming upon something new, the introvert says, "What does this mean in relation to me?" An extrovert asks, "How do I relate to this?" Introverts work to *assimilate* new information into their worldview; extroverts will change their worldview to *accommodate* something new. If you give a gift of some tchotchke to an introvert, they will try to find a place for it in their home (at least for a little while). If you give the same tchotchke to an extrovert, they may rearrange their living space around it.

Jung recognized that most people are not that strongly introverted or extroverted, but that there is a tendency towards one or the other. He also recognized that most of us, hovering around the border between the two, move from side to side in different situations. Some people *are* strongly introverted or extroverted, and Jung pointed out that when they try to take on the role of the opposite orientation, they tend to do so clumsily and with an obvious overcompensation. Strong introverts can get brash and loud when they try to go with the flow in social situations (think of the quiet coworker who has a few too many at the office party), and extroverts can get morose when they look inwards.

We can begin to see how things get complicated with the inner/outer division. We can be on one side either strongly or weakly. We can cross over to the other side. Most importantly, the introvert and extrovert both recognize an inner and an outer world, and the difference is in their *relationship* to each.

As we know, astrology is focused on change. The planets never sit still and new conditions are constantly being created. We are presented with new configurations never seen before—a new chart is born in each moment. These changes are reflected in our lives, both within as subjective experience and without as events.

When talking about whether change comes from within or without, the division between inner and outer can be very tricky to sort out. But it isn't too difficult to see that some kinds of astrology are more focused on inner experience, or our subjective impressions, whereas others are more concerned with concrete events in the world, things that can be measured objectively, such as getting married or getting fired from a job.

Because the more inner-directed astrologies are often the more recent, there is a temptation to think of these as more advanced than outer-directed astrologies. That is *incidentally* true, I think, but it isn't *necessarily* true. Much of contemporary astrology is postconventional and is directed towards inner experience, but that is the result of many factors, and shouldn't be taken to mean that subjective astrology is always going to be more complex than objective astrology. Mundane astrology as presented by Richard Tarnas and other archetypal cosmologists certainly has the same range of sophistication and depth that psychological astrology has, for example.

Most astrologies, especially in the last few decades, have taken the time to position themselves with regard to this distinction, although we might have to read between the lines a little. Overall, determining the orientation of a type of astrology is fairly easy.

The issues start when we blur the lines between inner and outer orientations. Now, there's no reason why an astrology can't cross the lines and encompass both, but very few do so without slipping up. The result is often that an outer-directed, objective astrology (one that is primarily concerned with events) often takes a rather reductionist approach to inner, subjective experience, and vice-versa.

Let's look at an example or two.

Uranian astrology tends to be very focused on events, and Uranian astrologers are proud of their predictive abilities. But they also get into character analysis, and relate aspects and midpoints to personality. Now, I'm not saying they do a bad job with this—and for clients that are appropriately matched to them, I'm sure they do very well. But consider how rigid the character descriptions are, and how deterministic their approach. Are there not many subtle ways that Mars on the Jupiter/Pluto midpoint can manifest? In the approach to inner experience, Uranian astrology tends to treat our inner states *as though they were* outer events. In fact, it tends to reduce our complex inner world to the aspects in our chart. It's not that the Uranian assessments are necessarily *wrong*, but they can cause trouble if the astrologers aren't aware of what they are doing. It would be better for Uranian astrologers to say, at least to themselves, that their system bends them towards outer events, and when they work with subjective experience, they need to be more tentative and perhaps learn to generate more alternatives than are found in their books.

Psychological astrologers run into similar straits when they start talking about outer events. Often, they feel uncomfortable with questions about what's going to happen, if a client will get a job or win the lottery, and so on. Neither the strategy of downplaying the importance of events nor taking an educated guess is likely to be of much help to the client.

In both cases the answer lies in consciously making a decision, either to admit the limits of one's perspective and make this clear to the client, or to cross over to the other perspective with awareness of our limitations. The latter alternative requires a deep and ongoing evaluation of our own perspective, in an attempt to uncover our biases in interpretation. Such awareness will not remove the biases, but to the extent we are aware of them, we can at least try to course-correct in our interpretations. If we can develop and maintain that awareness, we can actually offer clients both perspectives.

A third possibility exists, however, and it is one that we will explore in coming chapters. It is the possibility that we can have an astrology that is not focused on either inner or outer experience, but on the essential meaning of astrological symbols. From this perspective, we can understand that astrological symbols will manifest not only as inner or outer experiences, but both. Now, obviously most astrologers already know this, and the main difference in approach is one of emphasis. As I've said, the real problems come not because astrologers don't know that there is both an inner and outer dimension to astrological interpretation, but because it is difficult to keep issues of perspective in mind in the consulting room.

The shift in perspective that is required for this third possibility is not difficult, but it is subtle and requires a bit of patience. We have to hold at bay for a time our desire to know how an astrological factor will manifest, and focus instead on its inherent meaning. From there, the next step is to try to recognize that situations or events create and reflect internal states, and internal states create and reflect external events. The astrological symbol is neither internal nor external, but rather *the underlying pattern of both*. In other words, astrological factors manifest simultaneously in internal and external ways.

Many people are going to be focused on external events, and that's fine. Others are going to look to astrology to help with understanding their personality dynamics and to aid in their personal growth, and that is also fine. But it is something of a mistake to think that astrology itself is limited to either of these approaches. Where we put our emphasis can vary due to our temperaments, the situation, and other factors, but we should understand that at some level both internal and external interpretations are open to us. We can transcend the distinction or we can choose one side of it, but we should be careful not to smudge the line so that we carelessly bounce from one side to the other without being fully aware of what we are doing.[2]

CHAPTER 5
SCIENCE AND ASTROLOGY

My initial intention was to cover the relationship of science and astrology in the next chapter, but the section on scientific astrology kept getting longer and more detailed. Eventually, I decided the topic needed its own chapter. So, rather than talking about science and astrology under the heading of scientific astrology, I've reversed things and put scientific astrology in this chapter.

It makes sense that there is a lot to say about science and astrology. The scientific paradigm has been the dominant mode of thought—and belief—in Western culture over the past few hundred years. Every other mode of thought has to reckon its position with reference to science, and to do so intentionally and explicitly is undoubtedly better than ignoring the issue and letting others fill in the blanks based on their own perceptions.

Let us start off with a basic statement that will frame everything else: *astrology, as practiced by the overwhelming majority of astrologers, is not a science*. Scientific astrology is an attempt to study astrology scientifically, and we will get to that later in this chapter, but scientific astrology can hardly be considered the typical approach among astrologers. I know that the original meaning of the word *science* was more inclusive than its current, more specific definition. Previously, a science was simply a branch of practical or theoretical knowledge, and astrology *could* be considered a science in that sense. But arcane definitions of science can at best have the effect of making astrology an arcane science, and that isn't going to be much help in the contemporary world. Today, a science is a branch of knowledge that specifically uses the scientific method. Astrology obviously does not use such an approach to investigate and expand its knowledge base, although as in any discipline there is a process of presenting an idea, testing, and evaluation within the community.

Let me be clear that although I am going to point out many issues when it comes to astrology and science, I don't think that it is impossible to have a scientific approach to astrology. What can be done through such an approach will be limited, and I will show why, but that doesn't mean that it cannot provide valuable insights.

There are a variety of problems with taking a scientific approach to astrology, and they are all rooted in the radically different worldviews of science and astrology. Although the scientific worldview is not necessarily materialistic (it has been applied to a variety of non-physical topics, as the social sciences demonstrate), modern science began with and has had its greatest successes within the realm of the material world, and this has led to a materialist bias throughout much of the scientific community. For that reason, it is probably better to look towards the New Paradigm disciplines that are emerging than towards the materialistic scientific paradigm that has reigned over the last few centuries. Yet Bruce Scofield was right when he said that we might be too quick to reject that which has rejected us, and that the result is often careless thinking about astrology and how it works. It is therefore important to address the relationship between mainstream, materialist science and astrology.

Let's begin with a closer look at the divergent worldviews of science and astrology. Part of the scientific method involves testing a hypothesis, and measuring the results. For much of science, the acid test of scientific proof is *statistical significance*. Whether the phenomenon being measured reaches statistical significance determines if a drug will make it to the pharmacist's shelves, if the government will advise us not to eat salmon, if high-tension power lines can go over our houses, and most of the other findings we take to be scientifically proven.

Now, open any statistics book and within the first chapter you will find out that statistical tests have a very specific function, and that is to help us determine if a particular outcome was due to an actual relationship between two factors (for example, a drug and improvement of a medical condition) or if it was due to chance. If a phenomenon reaches statistical significance, it is unlikely that the result was a coincidence. Different scientists working in different contexts use various criteria for making that determination. Psychologists and other social scientists usually accept a finding if the odds of it being due to chance are less than 5%. Clinical research, as in medicine, often uses a higher threshold, typically around 10%, in part because it is hard to control for all the many factors that come into play (and probably because millions of dollars are being spent on the development of the drug).

Think for a moment about what statistical significance means: that an observed relationship between two factors was not due to chance, or, in other words, that the apparent relationship was not a coincidence. Now think about astrology, and how we approach the relationship between the heavens and our lives: *as above, so below*; the stars indicate, they do not impel. Many astrologers use the term *synchronicity* to describe how astrology works, and synchronicity is a term that describes *meaningful coincidences*. Statistics, and by extension much of science, is aimed at showing that relationships are not coincidences, but most astrologers make no such claim. It is not that what we observe are not coincidences—they are!—but that the coincidences are *meaningful*.

Demonstrating causality is not always possible due to limitations of research design, but scientists are generally aiming to uncover causal relationships rather than mere correlations (it would be good to know that taking the drug actually *caused* an improvement). Here again, we have a direct contrast with the synchronistic approach, because as the title of Jung's essay says, synchronicity is *an acausal connecting principle*.

What this shows is that astrology and science are working within two different paradigms. That paradigmatic difference will remain even if we try to show that the relationship between astrological and terrestrial factors is correlational rather than causal. Of course, if you do take a causal view of astrology, this isn't going to be a problem, but then you're going to have to explain why the planet Uranus has a particular effect on the psyche of humans and animals and terrestrial events, and a symbolic effect at that.

If we live in a world where science has been elevated to the status of a religion, it's no wonder: from the air conditioners that keep us cool to the jumbo jets that can ferry hundreds of people across the globe in less time than most people spend at work each day, we have the tangible evidence of the benefits of scientific thought all around us, all the time. It is also true, however, that science has led to a rather materialistic view of things and a tendency to see the world as "disenchanted" (as Richard Tarnas says) or as inert matter. There are extraordinary excesses, such as the view that reduces consciousness itself to an epiphenomenon of matter. These problems are important for astrologers, because a densely materialistic view of the cosmos makes astrology as most of us know and practice it impossible. Indeed, that is the primary reason why there is very little enthusiasm for studying it scientifically.

A few brave souls have endeavored to try to develop a scientific astrology, with mixed results. The most notable success is probably the work of Michel Gauquelin, who worked from the 1950s through the 1980s. His studies had a variety of interesting findings, including those that showed a relationship between planetary placement and career. Despite the excitement surrounding these statistically significant and oft-cited studies, they stand without much additional support. The lack of follow-up studies isn't the fault of astrologers, but we have to recognize that in no scientific field would forty- or fifty-year-old research stand as cutting edge. It is generally the practice that significant studies will be replicated, and that various independent variables will be manipulated in order to expand and refine the findings of a study.

Practical considerations limit the potential of scientific astrology. Even the modest budgets of a university's most esoteric departments must seem huge compared to the allotment of cash available for astrological studies. Much of the research must be done at home, on off hours, rather like a hobby.[1] The scientific community may scoff that there is no real scientific foundation for astrology, but they certainly aren't bending their resources to address the problem. That there are few supportive studies of astrology may simply be a reflection of the fact that there are so few studies at all: you cannot say for sure that your hat is not in the closet when you haven't taken the time to look. But as I said, a densely materialistic view of the world makes astrology impossible a priori, and to look seriously at astrology is usually perceived as a challenge to that materialist view. For materialistic science, that is as great a threat as Galileo was to the Church hundreds of years ago.

There are also significant theoretical problems with the scientific study of astrology. As early as 1936, in *The Astrology of*

Personality, Dane Rudhyar described a series of issues that would confront any attempt to see astrology as a science. Although he felt that it was a valuable project to look for statistical correlations of astrological and terrestrial factors, he recognized that such a project would ultimately be limited. Statistics, Rudhyar understood, measure the tendencies of groups, whereas astrology is focused in the other direction, on individuals. A particular astrological factor may be more prevalent in a certain group (e.g., athletes) but that does not mean that it is necessary for success within that group, or that its absence would prevent success. Rudhyar's sensible insights into the relationship between astrology and science continue to be valuable contributions to our understanding. A few more theoretical points are worthy of consideration.

Science became so materialistic because in general it has been great at measuring and manipulating the physical world, but it has a spotty record as soon as the same techniques are applied to the distinctly human sphere.[2] There are few principles in psychology and sociology that would be as universally accepted as the laws of thermodynamics, for instance. Part of the problem is having a clear idea what you are measuring. Although the human element is not entirely out of the picture when we measure something like temperature, there is a lot less room for variation than when we talk about a nebulous concept such as *motivation*.

Psychologists get around this by creating *operational definitions*. Essentially, a psychological researcher will say, "We can think of thousand different ways to look at 'motivation,' but for the purpose of my study I am going to define it by the number of widgets a person assembles per hour, and we can argue about its applicability to other situations later on." The result, on a good day, is a study that has decent validity in that it at least seems to measure what it claims.[3] The problem is that astrology is not only *conceptual*, but *symbolic*.[4] *Motivation* is a word that stands for something, although it may be hard to peg down exactly what. *Pisces* is a symbolic reference, and symbols are productive. That is, there is always another possible manifestation of Piscean energy: it can't be limited or operationalized. Consider also how we phrase astrological meanings. We say that if something is initiated when the moon is void-of-course, *it will not turn out as planned*. How shall we operationalize and measure *as planned*?

Scientists work with controlled conditions. Ideally, in experimental conditions, only one or two independent variables change. For example, two gardens may be planted next to each other, prepared with the same dirt, given the same fertilizer, and then planted with seedlings randomly selected from a large group. In every possible way, the two gardens will be similar. Then one garden is given a measured quantity of extra water in comparison to the other garden. The dependent variable, the growth of the seedlings, as measured by height or some other factor, is then compared. Because every other known factor has been controlled, we can assume that any differences in the plant growth are due to the difference in watering.

In real world studies, such as clinical trials, it is much harder to control for all possible factors. If scientists want to find out if women who eat more greens are less likely to have heart problems, they will need a very large sample, because among the women in each of the two groups (those who eat more and less green vegetables) there will be all kinds of confounding variables. Within each group, there will be variations in how much meat the women eat, how much exercise they get, family history of heart disease, and many other things that may have an influence on the study's outcome. Some factors, like family history, might be factored out either statistically or by excluding certain potential participants, but a long-term study like this would inevitably involve a number of confounding variables.

Astrology cannot be approached experimentally. We can't hold the positions of all but one planet constant and so observe that planet's effect in isolation from the others. In fact, not only are possible confounding variables always present, even the independent variable is in constant motion, and so not only experimental studies but correlational studies are going to be affected. No matter how we design a study, we will always be carrying it out in a dynamic environment where conditions are never repeated. If we do a study this year, we can't replicate it a year or so from now, because even if we have the same positions of one or two planets, others celestial bodies will have changed their relationships. And we can never know for sure if a planet can be discounted: for example, Jupiter and Saturn may not have much to do with a study of the relationship of Mars to Mercury, but they do have to do with science and the way we study things. That is, they will affect the scientist, if not the study.

The same problem of finding a steady platform from which to study astrology also applies to astrological symbols themselves. They are never seen in isolation, but always in some kind of relationship to each other. For most astrologers, this includes things like sign and house placement as well as aspects. There is never just the moon: there is the moon in a sign, the moon in relation to the other planets, and usually the moon in a house. These relationships are constantly changing, creating diverse symbolic pictures that cannot be understood in isolation unless we truncate much of astrology.

None of this means that the scientific study of astrology is impossible, but it does suggest that the best means of approach might be with the qualitative techniques used in the social sciences, at least as a complement to quantitative methods. For example, we could ask a group of people to describe how they felt at the time when they were having a significant Pluto transit, then compare their language to that describing a Jupiter or Uranus transit. Results could even be coded and statistically analyzed. There are many ways to approach scientific research in astrology, but efforts to show that a strong Mars will result in a surgeon, athlete, or butcher are likely to come up short.

There is so little scientific astrology around that it is hard to speak of a trend of any kind. Nonetheless, it makes sense that scientific astrologers would want to establish astrological principles based on their own data rather than on astrological tradition, and that seems to be the direction that is taken most often. In other words, rather than testing existing astrological ideas scientifically, scientific astrologers will look for greater-than-expected occurrences of some astronomical factor (say, Mars in a particular part of the chart) within a population, and then derive meanings *from* the data rather than trying to match the data *to* a preconceived idea about what it should mean. Using this approach, a scientific astrologer would be comfortable declaring that professional rugby players tend to have a strong Venus, if that's what the data says, just as Gauquelin was comfortable saying that Mars was strong in cadent houses.

That's a fine approach for scientific astrologers to take, and it may yield good and useful information for scientific astrology. However, we need to be careful not to fall into the trap of thinking that because an astrological idea has been derived scientifically it is necessarily any *more* valid than those that come to us through other means. I've heard many astrologers gushing over scientific verification of astrology, as though that somehow makes astrology more real. I can understand the feeling, given the high prestige of science and the low status of astrology, but there are problems. Most importantly, because scientific astrologers tend to start from scratch, they necessarily leave out much of the symbolic richness of astrology.[5] The complex, multiple meanings that are interwoven by a simple phrase like *Jupiter in Pisces* have to be discarded until reconstructed by the data. But as I have already pointed out, that is not likely to happen because symbols don't lend themselves to scientific study due to their ever-productive nature.

Scientific astrology, as it is currently formulated, is likely to yield a particular type of correlation between astronomical factors and some terrestrial manifestation.[6] Beware of claims that what is found via this approach is more valid than other forms of astrology. I'm not saying that it is any *less* valid, but rather that the types of meaning that can be derived from these techniques are limited. Why that is so will become apparent in a chapter or two,[7] but for now it is important to recognize that scientific astrologers are coming from a postconventional, scientific (and somewhat materialistic) approach, and as great as their results may be, they are going to have the greatest validity within that band of reality. And good results within one stage of development will not necessarily transfer neatly to others stages.

CHAPTER 6
FATE, FREE WILL, KARMA, AND CONSCIOUSNESS

This chapter contains some ideas that are crucial to developing an integral astrology, but they aren't astrological ideas per se. They therefore serve as a kind of background to the material in the next chapters. Still, I have related astrological information into these concepts as much as possible, and the ideas are sufficiently interesting in themselves to be worth a careful read.

Consciousness

Consciousness is essential to the cosmos, just as much a part of being as matter.

That statement might seem obvious, but for a good part of the last two hundred years it has been the subject of controversy. With the advent of the Scientific Revolution, we got very good at measuring the physical world. So good, in fact, that in the West we became overly enamored with our measurement device, the scientific method. The scientific toolbox includes all kinds of clever tools like the various research designs (experimental, descriptive) and statistical tests. These tools have allowed us to measure the material world and help us to get a handle on how it works. Science gave us cold beer on a hot summer's day, and you can bet I'm not complaining. But as I said in the previous chapter, the tools that we use to measure and understand the physical world work less well as we go up the ladder of evolution and try to understand the psyche, soul, and spirit. Consciousness is a particular bugaboo for science as it can't easily be measure with the same tools as material things, and for a while it wasn't even under scientific consideration.[1]

Each level of being, matter to life to self-awareness to soul to spirit, is more complex than the levels below it. You might be dealing with the same stuff, like atoms and molecules, but they are organized in increasingly complex ways. At the very least, that ought to mean that the measurement devices also need to become more complex. Science has tried to handle the increasing complexities, but the techniques that work at the basic physical level are so highly valued that they are held onto a bit too tightly at higher levels. The *scientific method* might be used successfully, but techniques to measure physical properties will most likely be inappropriate if something like feelings is the topic of concern.

The limitations of psychology have already been pointed out. By the time we get to something hugely complex, like macroeconomics, everyone realizes that *laws* are very provisional. What's more, it is apparent that humans and societies and other things at higher levels of organization are capable of change and transformation, so that a law that predicts behavior today might not hold true tomorrow.

The upshot is that the method that is so good at measuring the physical world tends to be only so-so at measuring more complex processes. Like a really accurate, laser-engraved titanium yardstick that can't reliably measure the circumference of a tree, the scientific method has yielded mixed results when applied to things like thoughts and feelings.[2] Over time we somehow came to the bizarre conclusion that if you can't measure something accurately with our wonderful tool, it must not exist. Since the physical world is there to be measured, we know it exists. Love, thoughts, sensations, values, and all the rest of the things we live for, got pushed out of the picture. By the middle of the 20th century, the dominant school of psychology in both the United States and the Soviet Union (less so in Europe) was behaviorism. Behaviorism was a unique kind of psychology, because it basically denied the existence of the mind, creating a situation kind of like a geologist saying there is no such thing as rock. Behaviorists admitted that something like the mind *appears* to exist, but they denied any importance to it, and instead focused on behaviors, which can be measured.[3]

Now, when psychologists start saying there is no such thing as mind, you've got an issue. But that was somehow an acceptable idea, at least in academic circles, and in a good deal of popular culture, too. Everything and everyone was seen as just a kind of machine. All of the things we care about and all of the experiences we have are just mechanical processes, inputs and outputs, and the reality of them is at the physical level. Behaviorists weren't the only ones to jump on the bandwagon, although they were perhaps the most obvious. If you fall in love, the behaviorists were ready to say it was because of a stimulus-response reaction that reinforced a particular mating behavior. Biologists were ready to say it was a link-up of pheromones while you are in a hormonal drive state. Geneticists were sure that it was your genes telling you that you had found a good match to help reproduce your chromosomes. And so on.

Those perspectives aren't entirely wrong, of course. A whiff of pheromones at the right time might serve to get your attention, and many of the things we find so attractive in individuals, particularly physical features, might have some underlying species-preserving genetic value. But falling in love is *experientially* distinct from any of the material factors we could ever associate with it. Yes, there may be some region of the brain that lights up when we are in love, but that doesn't mean that we experience love as an increase in bioelectrical activity.

It's a big topic, and I don't want to go too deeply into it here, because it has been covered elsewhere.[4] The basic point is that we got so good at measuring the physical world that we decided it was the only thing that really exists. Even the most powerful and obvious internal experience was reduced to a material process. Consciousness was not in the picture.[5]

If there's no such thing as mind, you can bet there's no soul or spirit. Mind is after all something that is at least apparently existent in our everyday reality. You have to work, as the behaviorists worked, to show it doesn't exist. But soul? A transcendent aspect to consciousness that is not dependent on the physical body? Have you actually seen such thing? Have you even experienced it?

Actually, the answer is quite possibly "yes." Through prayer, meditation, psychedelics, near-death and out-of-body experiences, and other means, many people have experienced transcendent consciousness. Materialists are quick to try to reduce such experiences to brain abnormalities, thus rendering them into hallucinations or delusions. After all, if consciousness has no real inherent reality, it's no big deal that a few extra neurons firing in the right temporal lobe can create an atypical version of it. Since your mind's existence is only a kind of illusion in the first place, an epiphenomenon of matter, what's the big deal if that illusion wiggles around a bit?

To answer the materialist perspective, there is a wealth of data that has been carefully accumulated over the past hundred years or so. Solid and respectable scientists have studied psychic and anomalous phenomena carefully, and some have run very tightly controlled studies in the area of parapsychology. These scholars include William James, often regarded as the father of American psychology. There are also verified stories of past life experiences, out-of-body experiences in which a person is able to tell what happened in other places, and many other kinds of evidence that show that consciousness can exist apart from the body. Because it doesn't fit well with the scientific-materialistic viewpoint, much of this evidence is ignored, even when it comes from a source with an excellent reputation. In fact, many scholars avoid doing such research because no matter how solid one's credentials are, you are likely to be seen as a member of the lunatic fringe for even investigating something like past life experiences.

Whether we are talking about everyday consciousness or a transcendent consciousness capable of existing outside of the body, we ought to be able to agree that consciousness exists, because it is manifest. You *are* conscious. The evidence is right here, right now. We don't really need to argue from the extremes or talk about out-of-body experiences if all we want to do is show that there is such a thing as consciousness. There is a lot of value in those special cases because they point to answers to the big questions of life. But that we are conscious ought to be obvious enough.

The materialist viewpoint didn't give much credence to consciousness, but the basic idea was that to the extent that it exists (or appears to exist), it must be dependent on matter. That seems to make sense if we look back over the course of history. Consciousness comes into the story fairly late, and self-aware consciousness even later than that.[6] When something unfortunate happens to the physical body, like a stroke or a dementia, consciousness often appears to contract, and at death it appears to cease to exist (or appears to cease to appear to exist, if you're a materialist).

Now, if we can recognize that consciousness is part of existence, we can start to think about how it relates to the physical world. An alternative view to the materialist approach is *idealism*, which puts consciousness first. Recall that in many evolutionary schemes there is an involution—spirit to soul to mind to matter—followed by an evolution in the opposite direction. In these models, consciousness, or a kind of superconsciousness, hides itself in matter, splitting itself into many individual shards of awareness, and then only gradually works its way back to completeness. Matter is the lowest level of existence, because it is consciousness unaware of itself. Our individual journey up the ladder of evolution is also the Godhead's journey back to itself, and when the path is completed it (we) recognizes that it (we) never really left. In these scenarios, matter is the more illusory partner, whereas consciousness is primary.

Yet another viewpoint has matter and consciousness as equal partners in the process of creation. In fact, they are not really two partners at all, but two sides of the same process. Matter is the outside, and consciousness the inside.

Each of these viewpoints has many variations. Some approaches, like Gnosticism, take a much darker view of the material world than scientific materialism takes of consciousness.[7] Many traditions, from Hua Yen Buddhism to Kabbalah, stress that at the end of the journey we will recognize nonduality, the resolution of the apparent dilemma.

Astrologers can approach this as they like, and our art is practiced well within the framework of duality. What we need to recognize is that consciousness is endemic to the cosmos, just as much a feature of existence as matter. If we believe that consciousness is entirely dependent on matter for its existence, we are going to find it hard to defend the idea that something like astrology can work, because consciousness can then only react to material conditions. In other words, all meaning would have to be created in our minds (or brains, for a materialist) as a result of sensory impressions. The empiricist perspective says exactly this: our brains provide the limiting framework for understanding sensory impressions, out of which we create meaning. Meaning, then, would have to be all in our heads. That could possibly work if we are talking about building a house and perhaps constructing a fair political system, but it would make astrology and in fact all of spirituality impossible (it also places quite a bit of stress on each of us—individually carrying all the meaning in the cosmos within our skulls). Astrologers are going to need to have either a *consciousness first* or *consciousness-and-matter-together* cosmos.

You cannot logically prove any of the alternatives (go ahead and try), and you can't whip out your scientific tools, either (for reasons we've already covered). All you can do is to gain some experiential understanding of the matter. You can then show that it isn't "just in your head" by talking to others who have had similar experiences, and you can verify and cross-validate each other. It won't convince materialists, of course, but then again nothing will. It won't lead you to any iron-clad conclusions, either, in part because the cosmos is always evolving and our understanding with it, and in part because our dualistic minds can only go so far in explaining the nondual experience.

It is only if consciousness is an integral part of the cosmos that astrology, along with any number of anomalous and nonphysical phenomena, can have any validity. The world of meaning and the world of matter must be riding on the same track for the kind of correspondences we see to exist. That we have to rely on mystical states and other anomalous experiences, or at least our inner experience, to support this should really take nothing away from it. After all, the tighter you define ordinary reality the more experiences will fall outside of it, and if the physical world is the only reality, then most of internal experience will be considered unreal.

As I said in the first chapter, there are many new scientists who are very willing to give consciousness a seat at the table, but there is often some subtle hierarchy involved that gives material existence a bit of an edge on consciousness. Astrology assumes a correspondence between matter and mind that exists at all levels: *as above, so below*, and that is apparently a hard pill to swallow unless you are really willing to give consciousness, not just *information*, equal billing.[8] Astrologers should at least know what kind of worldview is necessary for their discipline to have any validity.

Fate and Free Will

Answering the question of whether fate determines the course of our lives or if we have free will has been on the top of philosophers' to-do list for millennia. In fact, the question of how much control we have over our lives and how much is predetermined is one that makes amateur philosophers out of most of us. It is particularly relevant to astrologers and anyone who practices the mantic arts, because we do predictive work. Liz Greene wrote an entire book on the subject for astrologers, in which she relied heavily on Jung's understanding of the issue.

The typical approach the question of whether fate determines the course of our lives or if we have free will is to try to answer the questions as though the answers are out there somewhere, waiting to be discovered. There is a quantum of free will (or maybe there isn't) and a quantum of fate (or perhaps not), and we have to figure out how much of each exists. What few people have really considered—or have even been able to consider until recently—is the developmental aspect of this question.

We can elaborate in a bit, but for now, the answer is simple: fate and free will *are not givens*, they are *evolutionary*, like everything else. It is not a matter of there *being* fate and/or free will, as though they are objective conditions that exist apart from the subject. Without a good developmental model, we are left to try to figure if there is some kind of fate at work in the universe, or whether we have free will, or if there is some admixture of the two. Most people wind up deciding that there is some fate and some free will, but they don't have a clue as to why that is the case, or in what proportions they exist. Neither do they see why some people, in some areas of their lives, are apparently locked into fate, while others appear to be quite free.

Mystics have done a better job of explaining it than philosophers, because mystics understand that the real issue is transforming your self, not decoding the riddle logically. They know the answer lies in subjective awareness, not in objective circumstances. But that isn't a satisfying answer to a philosopher, and until integral theory was able to bridge these two approaches, mystics just seemed too irrational to really listen to.

The lower the level of development, the more fate is operative. For an organism that has only one option for action, external circumstances will dictate every motion. It's like pushing the power button—the machine has no choice but to go on or off. As we go up the developmental ladder, we have more options for actions, and free will becomes operative. It might sound as though that is being too simplistic, but it is the way things operate. For someone locked into a conventional, conformist viewpoint, there are only two options, do the right thing, or live with shame, guilt, and internal and external punishment. Go down a couple of levels to Purple, tribal consciousness, and there is only one option for action: follow tradition. But move up to an Orange, achievement-oriented postconventional approach, and there are literally infinite options, although only the ones that appeal in terms of one's values will really stand out. Few saints and bodhisattvas have much interest in astrology, so we won't be seeing many of them in our consulting rooms, but the report from the highest levels of consciousness evolution is that even physical laws can be bent and broken when consciousness becomes sufficiently self-aware. At the highest levels of development, even the duality of fate and free will, along with all the other dualities, is seen as illusory.

So, it isn't a matter of there *being* fate or free will. We *create* free will in the process of consciousness evolution. You can probably recognize that in the areas of life where you have a great deal of awareness and competence, you feel in control, whereas in those areas where you have your sore spots, blind spots, and sensitive spots, you are at the whim of circumstance. There are physical, psychological, and metaphysical dimensions to this, but at every level the same basic tenet holds true: awareness creates freedom.

The implications of this understanding for astrologers are enormous, of course. The whole question of prediction takes on a new, vertical, dimension when seen in light of consciousness evolution. We can see, for example, why old-timey astrologers were more focused on prediction: they lived in a world that should be predictable because there were few options for action available. Again, it isn't merely the case that there were few options *recognized*, but rather that until consciousness evolved to a certain point that allowed people to break free from convention, those options *literally* did not exist, at least not for most people. It also explains why it is still easier to make predictions for a group of people, like a nation or a corporation, than for an individual: it is much easier to accurately gauge the developmental level of a group, and groups are unlikely to surprise you with developmental leaps. A good many groups, from countries to governments to companies to other institutions, function at conventional levels or below much of the time, thus they are more likely to have predictable paths.

The real cut-off point in prediction is between the conventional (Blue in Spiral Dynamics) and postconventional (Orange in SD) levels. We'll see how this works in a practical way in a later chapter, but for now we need to recognize a qualitative difference between the conventional and postconventional worldviews, and then use that as our barometer for prediction. Consulting astrologers will notice right away that clients with a strong identification at the conventional level will want to know *what is going to happen?* Those operating from a postconventional perspective will want to know *what can I do about this situation?* A bit further on, the question might be *what does this mean?*

Fate has several levels of meaning. Those at the preconventional level typically see fate as a facet of life that is unalterable: one's path in life is predetermined and there is nothing to be done about it. It is like being caught in a sealed maze with the Minotaur: you can make all kinds of turns and run as fast as you want, but sooner or later your doom will catch up with you. Much of life remains up for grabs, however. At the conventional levels, fate is more about an impersonal force, a universal law. There may or may not be meaning involved at this level, because the universe works in an orderly fashion, proceeding from a first cause and following fixed laws. We more or less become cogs in a machine, although we might give thanks for the opportunity if we believe it is God's machine. At this level, all you can do is play your part, and if it turns out that you are assigned a role you don't like, you'll have to learn to live with it.[9]

Even those who believe in unalterable fate, however, have at least some sense of a limited free will. Preconventional societies have rituals that indicate they are taking part in keeping the universe in harmony, and through the intervention of the gods one might even be able, on a rare occasion, to escape one's fate. Conventional societies must assume free will even if it goes against a belief in an infallible process (mechanical or theistic), because one of the great joys of thinking you have found a universal truth is in the decision to live in accord with it.[10] Christians up until the Reformation were prone to saying that we each have a bit of God's free will at our disposal. If nothing else, a rigidly conventional viewpoint will have to admit that there is quite a bit of apparent variation and deviation from any natural way or ordered universe we think we perceive.

Once we get to the postconventional levels, possibilities start opening up rapidly. Prediction becomes very tenuous for someone who has options. As the Universal Way and Highest Truth starts to look relative, we can find whole new approaches to any situation. Thus we begin fated, and gradually our free will emerges as we increase our awareness and identification with ever-larger wholes.

Karma

There are volumes upon volumes that have been written about the law of karma, from both Eastern and Western perspectives. In the field of astrology, Stephen Arroyo and Steven Forrest have made extraordinary contributions to the discussion about astrology and karma, including the topics of awareness and even levels of consciousness. My goal is to correlate what they have said with developmental theory, because I believe it will be helpful to put their work in the context of a more explicit evolutionary schema.

The concept of karma has worked its way into Western culture over the last few decades, and those at various levels of consciousness perceive it in a way that makes sense to their particular viewpoint. Astrologers do not have to talk about karma, but many do. It is closely related to the question of fate and free will, and we'll see that it can be answered in more or less the same way.

At root, karma means *action* in Sanskrit, and the implied meaning is that our actions have consequences. It is a term that is closely associated with both Buddhism and Hinduism. The *Dhammapada*, an early Buddhist text, says that who we are today is the result of our thoughts of yesterday, and who we are tomorrow will be the result of our thoughts today. The text stresses that our lives are the products of our minds; it emphasizes a cause and effect relationship between thought and action. The Hindu *Bhagavad-Gita* is perhaps the most authoritative text on karma, and it stresses a profoundly conventional approach to the matter, exhorting us to play with gusto our role in the cosmic game, although we should keep in mind that it is ultimately a game.

We need to recognize that karma is, like everything else, developmental. That is, there is a conventional karma and a postconventional karma, although because it involves a universal law, it is hard to see karma operating on a preconventional level (universal laws are only possible with the advent of conventional thinking). Considering how karma works, it seems a worthwhile endeavor to try to move ourselves into the postconventional ballpark as soon as possible. If there is a good reason for not hanging around on the lower rungs of the developmental ladder longer than necessary, karma is it.

Karma, as it is often thought of in the West, is a kind of cosmic balancing act. The simplest interpretation of karma is usually something like, "if you steal a pocketbook in this lifetime, someone will steal your pocketbook in a future lifetime." This is indeed a valid formulation of the law of karma. You will note that it is very conventional in nature: there is some unalterable universal law (convention) seeing to it that the scales of justice are balanced. In fact, *justice* seems to be the operative word for karma at this level. Good actions are rewarded, bad actions are punished. The only thing that separates karma from our Western view of heaven and hell is that with karma, actions are apparently rewarded or punished *in kind*. It is very similar to the code of Hammurabi, "an eye for an eye," although with karma we have the assurance that even if a person escapes justice in this lifetime, they will find it in the future, and no human intervention is necessary.

We can also see a kind of postconventional karma, the kind alluded to in the earlier statement from the *Dhammapada*. What we think and do in one moment will create our perceptions and our reality in the next. If you steal a pocketbook now, you will *instantly* begin living in a world of thieves, fearful of being caught, fearful of others stealing your stuff. In each moment, we have a choice as to how we will live, a kind of ongoing decision tree. Some moments are more momentous than others, but at each point in time we make choices that affect our present and future. John Lennon said that he wrote his song, *Instant Karma*, when he realized that karma is not only about what happens in the future, but that it is also instant.

Notice that no external universal law is needed to enforce this kind of karma. There are consequences to our actions, but we create those consequences, and they are also reversible by our own choices. In this view of karma, the reason we actually have our pocketbook stolen in some future life is that it serves to bring the consequences of our actions into full awareness. Yet if we can develop awareness of our actions and their consequences, we won't necessarily have to live out our karma on the material level.

Everyone seems to agree that at times we can escape the nastier, live-it-out side of karma. Once again, the escape hatch is defined by our developmental level. At the conventional level, this usually involves surrender to a higher power, who (assuming that power to be personal) will then resolve the karma through an act of *grace*. This is very similar to the idea of salvation in Western religion, although it is not so much karma that is resolved as sin that is absolved: but either way the problem is solved. The individual recognizes the unwavering universal law, submits to the system or individual that represents it, and so goes straight and receives a pardon for their actions.

In the postconventional formulation, it is not so much acknowledgement that we transgressed a universal law, but awareness of how our thoughts and actions have shaped our reality. That is, at the conventional level, we accept guilt for having broken a commandment (although we don't necessarily fully understand the reason for the commandment and the consequences of breaking it), and higher authority then forgives us. At the postconventional level, it is awareness itself that resolves the karma.[11]

Note what happens when we bring disparate parts of ourselves into awareness and integrate them into our sense of who we are: *we heal*. The root of the word *heal* is the same as the root of *whole*. By acknowledging and accepting parts of ourselves that we have rejected, we become more whole than we were before, and we can see from more than a simple ego-based perspective. For example, we can see the harm we did to the person we stole from, and experience the emotional pain and the consequences it had for the other person.[12] We become more conscious, and we move up the ladder of evolution. As a result, what had to be acted out as a drama at the level where we created the karma can be released symbolically at a higher developmental stage. Our awareness of our actions and the mental and emotional patterns behind them allows us the freedom to avoid compulsively acting them out again.

Reincarnation is closely related to the concept of karma. In fact, many of the ideas in this book imply that reincarnation is a reality, and although almost all of the central ideas could stand on their own without reincarnation, many of them (like karma) would require heavy retooling. The fate of our individual consciousness after death has been the subject of speculation for eons, and there have been many perspectives and beliefs, from eternal heaven or hell to nonexistence. Belief in reincarnation is not a prerequisite for participation in most types of astrology.

However, there is some very compelling evidence for past lives. For example, there is the prevalence across cultures, including those that were not in communication with each other, of the belief in prior incarnations. There are numerous cases of people (especially children) remembering the details of past lives, forming something like a scientific database of verifiable experiences. Although less compelling from a scientific point of view, there are also experiences that people undergo during past life regressions, in meditation, in psychedelic sessions, and spontaneously. These last make up an intense *experiential*, if not objective, argument for reincarnation, particularly because the experiences are often psychologically and even physically healing.

We should recognize that there is not a single belief system about reincarnation, and that the specifics vary across time and cultures. Within the Buddhist and Hindu systems, reincarnation represents a chance for evolutionary development in consciousness. Given that we are born into human form, we have the chance to cultivate our awareness and potentially reach a state of enlightenment that will free us from the suffering inherent in incarnate existence. This chance for a quantum leap in the status of our consciousness is dependent on the right conditions of existence prevailing. Animals, for example, do not have the awareness necessary for enlightenment, and even the gods are too preoccupied with pleasure to really make any real spiritual progress (existence looks too good to them). These traditional systems contain an evolutionary potential, although they often stress that one can devolve more easily than evolve, a reflection of the strong conventional component within them.

A more Western view of evolution is that we learn lessons within each lifetime, and proceed through various situations designed to test our progress within and across lifetimes. As an extraordinarily simplified example, we may spend many lifetimes living from the level of the first chakra. At some point, we advance to become centered at the second chakra, and so on up the ladder of development. In this view, although the overall trajectory of development is linear and upwards, within each lifetime and across lifetimes we will need to visit many aspects of existence, and in that sense it is more like filling in a picture than climbing a ladder. We can make a lot of progress in one area of life, only to realize we have neglected another. Devolution is unlikely, although we may have to spend some time clearing up past issues. This upwards-only view of reincarnation and evolution is closely associated with the ideas of Theosophy.

If we at least tentatively accept that it is possible that there is some continuity of consciousness across lifetimes, that there is an evolutionary trajectory in successive lives, and that the natal chart contains some clues to the meaning of this life, then it follows that the chart also describes past lives to some extent. It is not that the chart is necessarily retrospective, but that the moment of the beginning of this life is a natural step in the sequence of past lives. As with any journey, where you are now is a result of where you have been in the past. This is the view taken by most evolutionary astrologers, such as Steven Forrest, and it suggests a way that astrology can work in harmony with belief in reincarnation.

CHAPTER 7
ASTROLOGIES

When they learn that I'm an astrologer, some people are quick to assert that they don't believe in astrology; others announce boldly (or admit timidly) that they do. Either way, I cringe a little.

The very term *belief* suggests a number of problems for astrology. Besides the lack of critical thinking it implies, the word also leads to the misunderstanding that astrology is a single, monolithic system rather than a diverse group of approaches that share a few basic assumptions. Chief among those assumptions is that there is a relationship between the sky and the earth, and that knowledge of one can tell you something about the condition of the other. Beyond that, various systems of astrology may not have a great deal in common. The diversity of astrological systems is well known to astrologers, although exactly how to deal with this complexity can be unclear. Certainly, however, we can say that there is not one astrology, but rather a plethora of *astrologies*, and we should note that different practitioners have their own perspectives and ways of working within a given system (and sometimes within more than one system).[1]

If astrology were not suspect among so many sophisticated thinkers in the modern world, this would not be such an issue. Many disciplines have a similar diversity. Psychology is an incredibly diverse field, with numerous distinct schools. At the far ends of the spectrum, psychoanalysts and behaviorists are speaking such very different languages that it requires a stretching of the imagination to say that they both belong to the same discipline, and in fact they do not always accord each other that courtesy.

By contrast, astrologers have tended towards a more tolerant and inclusive view of the diverse approaches that make up their discipline. Most astrologers I talk to seem to have a sense that there are astrologies for different astrologers as well as for clients, and that when all is working well the client winds up with the right astrologer for them. However, there is value in developing a clear idea of what underlying principle is operating when clients finds their way to Vedic, Uranian, or psychological astrologers and are satisfied with the consultations they receive. In this chapter, we are going to begin the process of answering that question, by looking at some astrologies through the lenses we have explored in previous chapters.

Astrologers need a way to approach the various systems that exist within the larger community of astrology. Cordiality reigns until astrologers with different perspectives begin to debate a specific issue. I am a member of several discussion groups for professional astrologers on the World Wide Web. Members of these groups are from all over the world, and they represent many types of astrology and the cultures in which they are embedded. The conversations we have about astrology are quite lively, and that is appropriate and fun. Yet I notice how quickly many astrologers strain to show that their own particular perspective is *the* right one, and I find that troubling. *The moon's void is superstition!* one astrologer will assert, deciding that modern astrology needs to be free of such archaic baggage. *The outer planets have no bearing on an astrological chart!* another will proclaim, holding fast to tradition. If anyone were looking in from outside, it would surely seem that astrology is in internal disarray. Which astrologer should we listen to if we want to understand astrology?

The issue of understanding multiple astrologies is more crucial today than ever before. Although there has long been an understanding that astrology has been changed and modified over the centuries, there has never been the kind of opportunity to explore diverse astrologies that exists today. An astrologer a hundred years ago would have known that there were both older and different approaches to astrology, but thanks to translations and interpretations, an astrologer today can actually *practice* astrology from another era or a completely different culture. All it takes is access to an online bookseller (a very low threshold!) for a Western astrologer to gain at least a functional knowledge of Chinese, Mayan, or Ptolemaic astrology.

Beginning with the resurrection of astrology in the late 19th century, there seems to have been a belief among Western astrologers that in time we would forge a new, modern, astrology, freed from the baggage of the past. But by the time that Pluto went into Sagittarius (signaling the transformation of belief systems), the goal of a single, unified, modern astrology seems to have been replaced by a postmodern appreciation of the diversity of astrological perspectives. What remains to be done is to organize these various perspectives into a cohesive, multidimensional, integral astrological system.

We would do well to note that astrology in the last couple of millennia seems to have had a kind of complementary role in Western society. While the Church dominated spirituality in the Middle Ages, astrology was considered a natural science. As secular scientific thinking began to define the scene, astrology faded because it didn't really meet the emerging scientific standards. When it re-emerged in the 19th century, astrology became a metaphysical, spiritual discipline, compensating—along with other divinatory techniques, esoteric teachings, and "magik"—for the extremes of materialism. In the West, at least, astrology has been on the outside for quite some time.

Ostracism can create powerful effects, both negative and positive. Being on the outside of a group or society can create a perspective on that culture that is not easily seen from within. Outsiders can more clearly see the limitations and inconsistencies with which people live without reflection. Having an atypical perspective or value system not only gives insight into the benefits and problems of the norm, it also frees the outsider to act more independently and perhaps even more creatively.

But there are costs to being an outsider, and we have to be aware of these, as well. One common problem is a kind of counter-rejection, as Bruce Scofield pointed out. If a basically materialistic, scientific (or traditional religious) culture rejects astrology, astrologers might respond with a wholesale denigration of science (or religion).

Another problem is the difficulty of an outsider group to identify its own weaknesses. To the extent that astrologers are on the defensive with regard to the materialist perspective that dominates Western culture, there is a danger of closing ranks and hardening our own belief system. Defensiveness and openness are rarely seen together.

Significantly, those within the outsider group may exhibit a tendency to compete with each other. Being outside of the mainstream generally involves low prestige, and it is not uncommon for individuals to try to make up for that by becoming the top dog among the underdogs. That can be attempted in many ways, from proclaiming that one has the best or the true astrological system, to trying to show that one's system really should be considered part of the mainstream, or is at least closer to the mainstream than other systems.

In actuality, I do not often see these negatives in the astrological community. Despite some spirited disagreements, astrologers generally have a relatively mellow live-and-let-live attitude. Failing to earnestly discuss inconsistencies and incompatibilities is more of a problem than attacks. Still, there is a darker side to every community, astrologers included, and it is better to be aware of the issues than to ignore them.

Since I am making generalizations in this chapter that some may object to, let me be clear that I am speaking here of astrologies as they were more or less originally formulated or as they are best known. I fully understand that the techniques of a particular school may be used in different ways by different astrologers. For example, Robert Hand was demonstrating a postconventional perspective on astrology at least as far back as his popular book *Planets in Transit*, published in 1976. Throughout the 1970s and 1980s he developed a complex, choice-oriented approach that is typical of psychological astrology. In more recent decades, Hand has become interested in ancient and medieval astrological techniques that were popular during a time when most astrologers were operating at a conformist, conventional level of development. It would be wrong, however, to think that Hand has somehow regressed to an earlier stage of development, personally or in his astrology. In fact, as a reading of his work shows, he has an ability to shift back and forth among multiple astrological perspectives, noting the relative strength and weaknesses of each for a given situation. Similarly, Indian (or Vedic, or Hindu) astrology in its canonical form tends to be very fatalistic, but it would be a mistake to think that all practicing Vedic astrologers are themselves fatalistic in their astrological work.

In my estimation, most of the leading lights of astrology today are operating from a postconventional perspective, and at present the level of development has much more to do with the astrologer than the system he or she uses. A postconventional astrologer can use a conventional system of astrology, but will reinterpret it in postconventional terms—it would be hard to do otherwise.

There is value in looking back over the history of astrology to see how different astrologers and different systems of astrology have expressed various developmental and cultural perspectives. It will help us to answer critics of astrology, and to orient ourselves to astrology as we practice it now. To my knowledge, the first attempt to explicitly correlate various types of astrology with developmental levels of consciousness was made by Dane Rudhyar in his book *The Astrology of Personality*, in 1936. His survey effectively links the basic constructs of consciousness to the astrology that results from the operation of these constructs, and his book should be considered among the foundations of integral astrology.

The following is not intended to be any kind of comprehensive history of astrology, but rather a survey of what has gone before and what is on the scene now. The complex tapestry woven by the schools of astrology and the philosophies that informed them makes for a fascinating study—but one the reader will have to find elsewhere. For readability, I have been as brief as possible, but the notes and the sources at the back of the book have more information. As I am not an historian of astrology, there is bound to be some contention about the details of the individual systems, but the basic outline is sound in reference to the levels of consciousness development.

Early Astrology

Astrology is old enough that we cannot really find its roots. It appears for the first time in the historical record around the second millennium BCE, but it would seem probable that people were looking to the heavens for signs about coming events in the prehistoric era. The earliest records of Mesopotamian astrology, according to Robert Hand (who *is* an historian of astrology), are omens with significance for the king.[2] At this time in history, most people were at the Purple level of development, but Red was emerging in the person of the king. Astrology from this era is therefore uniformly preconventional. By the first centuries BCE, there were listings of planetary positions for birth times, something very like horoscopic astrology; these birth omens were not only for the king but for other people as well.

According to Hand, at this time omens were matched with rituals for propitiating the celestial forces in order to mitigate otherwise negative effects. This is an important point, because it demonstrates a preconventional attitude towards fate. For people operating from a preconventional level, there are external forces in both the natural and supernatural worlds that will have an impact on them. A person deeply entrenched in Purple probably does not see herself as separate enough from these forces to have much sense of individual potency *against* them, although the community as a whole performs rituals that are *in concert* with them. At the level of Red, the personal ego is developed enough to want to avoid potential dangers, and this can be accomplished by bargaining with the gods. We continue to see this today in the *upajas* of Indian astrology.

There is a very subtle difference between a programmed group ritual, such as a solstice rite in winter to bring the sun back to its heights, and an individual's ritual to alter the effects of an ill omen. Both may involve the same kinds of activities, such as animal sacrifice or offerings of food at temples, but the former reflects only the dimmest awareness that things could be other than they are, whereas the latter assumes a degree of bargaining power and an almost surprising sense of individual worth. However, both do assume that there are supernatural forces or personalities (ancestors, spirits and gods) with an independent consciousness of their own. In other words, at these levels, *there is free will in the universe*, although it is largely in the hands of the gods, and humans participate in it only indirectly.

Hellenistic Astrology to the Renaissance

With Hellenistic astrology, we come to the beginning of astrology as we know it today, with true horoscopic astrology in a fully developed and complex system. The complexity and variation by the time of the Hellenistic period of astrology, beginning in the first century CE, makes it beyond the scope of this book to treat the system(s) in any detail.

What is significant for our purposes is the association of astrology with various philosophical systems that assumed a rational and knowable order in the universe. Whereas the history of early astrology is relatively sparse until the Hellenistic era, the history of philosophy is rich and complex during the six or so centuries, BCE, in what is sometimes called "the axial age."[3] The thematic variations on philosophic questions are an interesting study, but one that we will have to approach by abstracting only the most basic common principles. By the time of Ptolemy, humans had differentiated themselves from both the physical and metaphysical worlds (they had formed egos) sufficiently that they could reflect on things and see patterns and phenomena as part of an abstract, transcendent system. The workings of the natural world became of great interest, and soon the very need for the intervention of the gods was called into question. The universe had a *way*, an operating principle or principles that formed some sort of orderly system to which even the gods had to conform. Mathematics seemed to hint at this, as did the observation of nature, the relatively new ability to think about thinking (metacognition), and the outlining of principles of logic.

At this point, much effort went into discovering and knowing these transcendent principles and learning to live in accord with them. When seen in its extreme form, the universal harmony would not admit of any changes whatsoever—everything in the cosmos throughout all time and space was arranged just so, and no modifications could disturb this order. The result was the emergence of conventional astrology.

Conventional astrology was and is very fatalistic. Of course, not all astrologers or versions of astrology at this point in time were at the conventional level, and even within individuals there is a tendency to mix various levels of development. The result may be an astrology that lacks self-consistency, but that is a relatively common issue in most human endeavors.

Yet astrology clearly changed. When preconventional thinking prevailed, the wandering planets were initially the gods themselves (perhaps), and before reliable ephemerides it was even thought that their orbits could vary at will. When they were known to follow a particular path—like the sun on his daily journey or the moon on hers—they were still following *their own* path. By the time of Newton, the planets were thought of as objects in the sky that were compelled in their orbits by gravity and the laws of motion. These laws of physics thus became the real powers in the universe. At first, a transcendent principle remained, in that God had created the universe and its physical laws. As many have pointed out, it was only a small step to dispose of God and leave only the laws of physics as the ultimate principles of reality. People saw the universe as a clockwork machine.

Conventional astrology's fatalism thus differs significantly from preconventional versions. In the Purple and Red preconventional worlds, there may be events in a person's life that are fated, or a person may be doomed to a particular role in life. But the fated parts of life are seen as relatively self-contained experiences. Oedipus, Agamemnon, and Odysseus all had their fates to contend with, yet they had a degree of freedom in their responses, and many aspects of their lives remained relatively unaffected. By contrast, conventional thinking results not so much in a vision of *fate* as a meaningful doom, but rather of *determinism* as the condition of existence. Since everything has a potentially knowable cause and effect, all of existence is simply the unfolding in time of the original set of circumstances. Existence is like a giant chain of dominoes, and all aspects of it are predetermined at the start.

Not all versions of conventional thought are quite as rigid as that which resulted from the Western fascination with the physical world and the sense of meaninglessness that accompanies it (after all, no power is assigning you your personal fate—it is all just a giant machine in which you are a cog). But most of conventional thought cites an overarching principle that cannot be violated. As Chris Brennan[4] has said, with belief in a predetermined universe, precise astrological prediction should be possible, and the various incarnations of conventional astrology are thus focused on prediction to the extent that they view the universe as determined.

If earlier preconventional astrology has saddled the field with an image of superstitions and omens, conventional astrology has caused us difficulty by maintaining that future events are in principle completely knowable if we but understand how our own system works. When most of conventional astrology was formulated, there was at least a parallel symbolic world in addition to our physical world, even if both were fixed and determined. As the scientific viewpoint took over, the symbolic, metaphysical world began to fade into the background and eventually disappeared for many people. That left astrologers in the awkward position of explaining astrology as either a physical system working on a causal basis (like chemistry or physics) or maintaining that the symbolic realm did in fact exist on its own terms. The first explanation has not been substantiated, and the second explanation was going to be unpopular for hundreds of years to come.

Astrology of this period was not fully deterministic. As I have said, there were many schools of philosophy active and changing in themselves and in their influence on astrology, and of course astrologers vary in their approaches even within a school. Another approach allowed for at least some free will; this grew out of a counter to deterministic (most notably Stoic) philosophy by the early Christian church.

The church was in a bind with the issue of free will and determinism. On the one hand, God had clearly set up an orderly and harmonious universe that should probably be considered perfect, as it was His creation. But on the other hand, if we live in a rigidly determined universe, there isn't much point in us *trying*. Salvation by belief in Christ as the savior is an apparent act of will, yet if we live in a determined universe, that salvation must already be knowable, at least in the mind of God.

That was a problem! Since God is omniscient, He (for He was always a "he" in the past) must be able to know whether or not you will be saved. In fact, He must know everything that will happen, and in that sense it must be predetermined. Therefore, you don't really have free will. In this version of things, it is not so much a matter of a clockwork universe as God's omniscience of his own creation. During the Reformation, this was a key point for Martin Luther, who believed just that.

Most Christian philosophers, however, took a view that maintained free will. Boethius addressed this dilemma in a way that was so far ahead of his time that I have to question whether he meant it in the way we take it today, when he said, "knowledge is a quality of the knower, not of the known." That is, what we know is based on our subjective position, from which we see the object of knowledge. What we know is not inherent in the object itself, but in our understanding of it. Climb up the ladder of evolutionary understanding, and when you get close to God, you'll see why you have free will *and* God is omniscient. Most philosophers and church officials didn't get quite so heady, though, and fell back upon the idea that God gave us each some free will to work with within His creation.

Having a bit of free will does nothing to change the conventional nature of these systems of philosophy and the astrologies that we associate with them. If we don't have free will, we are bound to every moment of our lives by an unyielding determinism. But if we do have free will, so these systems tell us, we can use it to follow the right way (God's will, the natural order, etc.) or to violate the principles of the good life. Indeed, the conventional worldview has no problem with free will; in fact, it prefers to believe that free will exists. After all, once we've identified the right choice, how much better it is to piously make it! And what would become of all the engines of guilt and punishment in this world and the next if there were not free will?

Conventional astrology from the Hellenistic period to the Renaissance thus included views that were completely deterministic and those that allowed for at least some free will. All of them, however, assumed an underlying order of some sort in the cosmos, whether it was a natural way of things, a scientific determinism, or God's will that served as the transcendent ordering principle.

Jyotish or Hindu (or Vedic), Indian Astrology

It is extraordinarily difficult to make much in the way of conclusive statements about an astrology that has been around for thousands of years. Jyotish, the "science of light" has existed in India for an amount of time almost equal to all of the Western astrologies combined. Ronnie Gale Dreyer has suggested that Jyotish is not directly linked to any particular philosophy,[5] but I think it is reasonable to say that it has been inextricably linked to many aspects of Indian philosophy and culture over the centuries.

For our purposes, it is important to recognize that Jyotish is regarded as being highly accurate in terms of prediction of major life events. Character analysis is also part of Indian astrology, and there is a strong linking of both life events and character to past lives, through the mechanism of karma.

Importantly, karmic events and personality traits can often be changed or at least ameliorated by actions, such as rituals. A client of mine was told by an Indian astrologer that her first marriage would be bad (there were indications that it would be challenging in her Western chart, too, for different reasons). To solve the problem, she performed a ceremony in which she was married—to a coconut. As predicted, the marriage did not go well, and was soon dissolved, leaving her ready for her more productive second marriage.

While modern Westerners might view this approach with skepticism, we should note that it does involve bringing the issue to consciousness and working with it on both an intellectual and, perhaps more importantly, an emotional level. We should also remember that Jyotish developed within the Indian cultural system, which produced sophisticated psychologies in the Hindu and Buddhist traditions centuries ago. Jyotish thus resonates, to varying degrees, with preconventional, conventional, and postconventional thinking and values.

Non-Western Astrologies

Astrology has been part and parcel of most cultures, including Chinese, Southeast Asian, and South American. Each of these astrologies has developed through an observation of the heavens from within a particular cultural matrix. In that way, it has reflected the culture and its evolution over time. Since the point of an integral astrology is not to catalog every type of astrology but to come to an understanding of a way to approach all astrologies, and since I am no expert in non-Western astrology, I will leave the particulars to interested parties, with the hint that many of these astrologies seem to me, based on casual knowledge, to have both preconventional and conventional elements within them.

Astrology in the 20th and 21st Centuries

The following are some of the generally accepted schools of astrology of the last hundred years or so. Astrology during this time has hardly been an academic discipline, and the divisions are based on agreed-upon demarcations within the field. Yet although it is perhaps a little easier to see that which is recent and still active with a clear eye, at times a very near object is just as hard to see as one that is in the distance.

Coming into the 20th century, astrology was just beginning to repair itself from the decline of the 18th century. Although the spirituality and Theosophy of the 19th century were part of this revival, it is apparent that many of the more enlightened aspects of these movements did not make it into the astrology books of the time, which tended towards fatalistic interpretations. I would suggest—and it is just a suggestion—that after more than a century of decline and neglect, it took some time for astrology to collect itself and move forward as a discipline, and so despite the best intentions of many practitioners it was initially presented in a rather antiquated form.

As we go through the various contemporary astrologies, keep in mind that astrologers today are exposed to many kinds of astrology, and are likely to use an eclectic mix of several schools. Also, note that scientific astrology has already been covered in the previous chapter, but it could and should be considered a separate school of (or at least approach to) astrology.

Uranian Astrology

Uranian astrology is a school unto itself. Unlike the hazy borders of psychological or traditional astrology, Uranian uses a specific set of techniques to yield a particular set of interpretations, and so is perhaps the most clearly demarcated type of astrology today. For many, Uranian is a system that favors concrete, event-oriented predictions, and this is certainly a part of the system. However, Uranian is also concerned with character, as Ebertin's popular book, *The Combination of Stellar Influences*, demonstrates. This acknowledgement of character and disposition as facets of astrology is in concert with other astrological schools of the 20th century. The formulations of Uranian therefore refer to both inner and outer events, but with a high degree of emphasis on what we might call astrodeterminism. Free will does not seem to be a prominent belief within this school of astrology, even when inner character is the concern.

In its trappings, Uranian astrology appears to be very clean and scientific. The use of the 90- and 360-degree dials, the limited influence of the archaic symbols of the zodiac and the complete absence of poetic expression in the system suggest a postconventional viewpoint. But the actual substance of Uranian astrology is strictly conventional, both in its emphasis on deterministic formulations and in the school's ongoing dogmatic references to the original sources. Ebertin's book has become something of a bible for this school, and Alfred Witte's initial revelations during the First World War have become the stuff of legend.

This is in no way meant to detract from the school. I am relatively certain that Uranian astrologers are nearly as accurate and precise as they claim to be, and that their techniques serve their clients well. The Uranian school was and is a significant development in the history of astrology. The use of midpoints seems to be a particularly important innovation. I am only concerned with locating the school within the context of the development of consciousness, and in that respect it is primarily conventional. As with traditional astrology, the emphasis on being *right* in terms of prediction implies that there is a predetermined outcome, and that is conventional thinking. Again, while Uranian astrology is conventional, I do not suppose that all Uranian astrologers are.

Psychological Astrology

As we know, the astrological literature of the last half-century or so distinguishes between externally focused, event-oriented astrology and internally focused *psychological* astrology. Because different astrologers in different epochs do tend to emphasize one or the other, this distinction is at least apparently valid. It would be something of a stretch, however, to state that the use of astrology for the understanding of character is an exclusively modern invention.[6]

I find the association between internal and external problematic when it links externally oriented event astrology with a fatalistic viewpoint, and psychological astrology with free will. Any serious perusal of the literature of psychology will show that that field is based on the assumption that internal events like thoughts and feelings are causally conditioned, just like external events. In fact, psychology could not have presented itself as a modern science if this were not the case.

In the physical universe, we might look to a billiard table for a simple example of causality. If one ball is about to crash into another and we know the mass of both and the velocity and direction of the moving ball, we ought to be able to predict the resulting motion of the second ball when it is hit. Psychology assumes that our internal states will follow similar rules, although of course it is difficult to measure thoughts and emotions as compared to physical objects. But from Freudian psychoanalysis through Skinnerian behaviorism, a central tenet of psychology has been that the human psyche is predictable and knowable in much the same way as the physical world. Thoughts, feelings, and other internal experiences are just as subject to causal determinism as anything in the physical world, they are just harder to measure.

Given that modern psychology did not develop until the 19th century, it is reasonable to say that psychological astrology as such could not have developed until around the same time, and except to the extent that astrologers are cutting-edge psychologists, probably a little later. That seems to be the case, and the attribution of the beginnings of real psychological astrology with Alan Leo and Dane Rudhyar in the first half of the 20th century[7] does describe the beginning of a self-consciously (excuse the pun) psychological astrology. This approach to astrology reached its peak—at least for the present—from the 1970s through the 1990s, with the works of Stephen Arroyo, Liz Greene, Donna Cunningham, Karen Hamaker-Zondag, and the early writings of Steven Forrest, among others. Many of the proponents of psychological astrology tied their work directly to the psychology of Carl Jung, and a good number of them were also professional analysts and counselors.

Psychological astrology could not have arisen until there was psychology, but the actual flavor of most of the prominent writings of psychological astrology demonstrates another development that was just as crucial. Although Rudhyar and Leo began writing in the first half of the 20th century, the astrology of personality and the emphasis on choice, free will, and internal experiences did not gain traction until the 1960s.[8] In that decade, there was a significant cultural movement up the ladder of consciousness, with the widespread emergence of the humanistic, postconventional Green Meme (via the Civil Rights and other movements, as well as by the widespread use of psychedelics). Until this emergence of postconventional worldviews on a large scale, there was little to pull astrology out of the conventional mode.

Psychology per se would not have done the job. Much of clinical psychology, it should be remembered, has the expressed goal of helping people to lead lives as normal, well-adjusted members of society. For all his groundbreaking postconventional work, for example, Freud's psychology is ultimately conventional in its aim. Jung's work was geared towards psychological wholeness, and that strongly suggests a postconventional worldview, because with the black-and-white thinking of the conventional level, shadow material cannot be accepted and incorporated into the self-image. The essential character of what is called psychological astrology is not only psychological, it is postconventional, as it is only at the postconventional levels that a self-reflective person can create new options for being. In fact, it might be more proper to refer to this kind of astrology as the postconventional school, or even more accurately, the humanistic school. Either would be more consistent with the emphasis on choice and free will that is characteristic of this approach.

I have mixed feelings about the term *psychological astrology*. On the one hand, I have a lot of respect for psychologists and their discipline, and the years of research that has come from its many schools. For astrologers to appropriate the use of the term seems a little presumptuous. Clinical psychologists also get a great deal of training in counseling and working with clients, something that is optional in the astrological world, and not very easy to find if you opt for it.

On the other hand, as psychology literally means the study of the soul, it doesn't seem realistic that any one profession would have exclusive rights to the name. I said earlier that astrology has acted as a kind of compensation for the dominant mode in Western culture, and that in the last hundred years or so it has represented the interior, subjective self in a material world. Psychology *almost* fulfilled this role, as the work of Freud, Jung, James, and many others show. However, in its bid to become more like the hard sciences, psychology gave up much of its emphasis on phenomenology and meaningful interior experience. That opened up the door for astrology and other esoteric disciplines to come in and fill up the gap. So, in a way, *psychological astrology* is a very valid term.

However I feel about the terminology, I recognize the extraordinary value that psychological astrology has for the discipline of astrology, for the clients it serves, and for our understanding of ourselves. Many works of psychological astrology parallel the great works of psychology in helping us understand the psyche.

In an interesting—and at this writing still ambiguous—change of direction, around the turn of the millennium the astrological community began to see a reemergence of the techniques of traditional astrology. *Project Hindsight* may have served as the proximal cause of the interest in prior astrologies, but it is unlikely that the translations and explanations that came out of that project would have had such an impact were there not other factors at work. This complex issue is left for the reader to ponder, although I will offer that perhaps some people have become disenchanted with the free will to be found in the postconventional world, and traditional astrology may offer a more certain view of the world. Still, I will say again that knowledge of traditional astrological techniques does not necessarily imply a conventional worldview on the part of the practitioner.[9]

Another possibility is that earlier astrologies were more technically demanding, and it has taken some time for contemporary astrologers to reach a point where they could get serious about the details of traditional systems. Recall that Ziphorah Dobbins was very influential in reducing astrology's language to twelve letters at the height of the psychological astrology movement. However, the most likely reason for the stalling of psychological astrology and return to traditional techniques, in my opinion, is that without the missing developmental component that makes the two dimensional chart into a three dimensional image, psychological astrology had gone about as far as it could.

Archetypal Cosmology

This is a school that has emerged very recently, centered at the California Institute of Integral Studies and at the Graduate Institute in Connecticut. As the academic associations imply, it is not so much a school of astrology as an academic discipline, although there are practicing astrologers who identify themselves as archetypal cosmologists.[10]

One of the key points of archetypal cosmology is that astrological symbols are *multivalent* and *multidimensional*, and thus can manifest at any level of existence, internally within an individual, externally in their lives, in our collective life, and so on.[11] Astrological symbols describe archetypal patterns, not specific manifestations, according to archetypal cosmologists, and the proper focus is not on exactly what will happen (or has happened), but on the deeper meaning of the archetypal interactions. Archetypal cosmologists frequently use the images of myth as a means of transcending the limitations of verbal astrological interpretations. In that sense, they point to the archetypal dimension that informs our spatiotemporal experience.

Archetypal cosmologists address natal configurations, personal transits, and *world transits*. Because they are represented thus far most prominently by Richard Tarnas' book *Cosmos and Psyche*, a significant work of mundane astrology[12], it is through the analysis of world transits that most people know archetypal cosmology. Astrologers will appreciate that Tarnas explains events in terms of aspects of the outer planets, but they will also note that he does not use signs.[13] He also uses twenty-degree orbs for aspects (ten degrees approaching and ten separating). *Cosmos and Psyche* thus presents significant departures from astrology as it is typically practiced.

At present, it is too early to assess the trajectory of archetypal cosmology. What is clear is that it is an attempt to present solid astrological material in a way that will be accepted by the New Paradigm disciplines, thus helping to secure for astrology the recognition I talked about in the introduction.

Evolutionary Astrology

Evolutionary astrology is closely associated with the work of Jeffrey Wolf Green and Steven Forrest; Forrest is one of the most prominent astrologers on the scene in the decades surrounding the turn of the millennium. More recently, Maurice Fernandez and Eric Meyers are among those who have added to the cannon of evolutionary astrology. Evolutionary astrology grew out of psychological astrology and is characterized by a more focused approach than its eclectic parent. Most evolutionary astrologers explicitly reference the work of Forrest and Green and see themselves as contributing an expansion of their foundational ideas.

Evolutionary astrology is also more explicitly spiritual than psychological astrology. There is a great deal of emphasis on past lives, although reincarnation is understood as part of a process of the evolution of consciousness over lifetimes rather than as a point of interest in itself. Forrest does not state that astrology is capable of illuminating the factual details of former incarnations with any precision, but rather that the natal chart—particularly the lunar nodes and aspects to them—create a valid *as if* image of a relevant past life and its continuing emotional influence.

To the extent that we live in a meaningful universe and astrology is a system to help illuminate that meaning, the natal chart must contain some clues not just to the conditions of a person's life but also to its meaning and the lessons that need to be learned. There is no necessity, per se, that past lives be brought into the picture, since on a purely theoretical level each of us could be a unique manifestation of universal energy and meaning with no particular continuity to the past.

Steven Forrest is quick to point out that the chart describes the kinds of challenges and opportunities the individual faces in this lifetime, and in kind they are related to past lives. However, he also stresses that the chart itself does not indicate the level of conscious awareness the person has—that is, it doesn't tell us about the developmental level. That is a subtle point that should not be overlooked: Forrest recognizes that the chart is a two-dimensional representation of relevant circumstances, both past and present, but the chart does not describe the conscious capacity to deal with those circumstances. In that, he follows Rudhyar and Arroyo in recognizing the value of astrology as a *tool* for evolutionary development rather than a *map* of the process.

That we have varying capacites for meeting challenges and opportunities implies a degree of free will, and Forrest nails the argument when he states that the degree of awareness one has (i.e., the developmental level) correlates to the degree of free will available. That is, the more aware we are, the more conscious we become, the more freedom we have in manifesting aspects of our natal charts and in responding to the circumstances created by transits.

That is an approach that was also taken up by Maurice Fernandez, an evolutionary astrologer whose book, *Astrology and the Evolution of Consciousness*, presented a nonastrological system of consciousness development together with astrological insights.[14] Fernandez then went on to give examples of how a particular astrological symbol like the sun in Aries can manifest at different developmental levels. The recognition that astrology interacts with the evolutionary process has already been established, but Fernandez made a helpful contribution by actually providing a three-dimensional model where the third dimension is dealt with explicitly.

A different approach was taken by Eric Meyers, another evolutionary astrologer, in *Elements and Evolution*. Meyers has a view of consciousness evolution that is in concert with developmental theorists, but he uses the four elements as a basis for understanding the process. Recall that the basic evolutionary scheme follows the pattern of matter to life to mind to soul to spirit. Meyers associates Earth with matter, Water with life (and emotions), Air with mind, and Fire with spirit (using the four elements means that he sees four levels as opposed to five, or seven, etc.).

Like the chakra system, it can be challenging to keep horizontal and vertical perspective distinct, because we all have each of the four elements operating in our charts, representing both developmental steps and energies that exist at each level. Just as we all have a fourth chakra, but an individual may be operating from a third chakra perspective, so we all have some Fire in our charts but might be operating from a Water or Air perspective. Meyers ideas include both the cyclical processes of the zodiac and the developmental process through the elements, creating a "spiral stairway" of evolution.[15]

Evolutionary astrology represents a true evolution of astrology in several respects, including most notably the acknowledgement of the importance of varying levels of consciousness in interpretation and the linking of astrology to a genuinely spiritual perspective.[16] This last point should be appreciated, because astrologers have generally been careful not to align themselves too closely with any spiritual or metaphysical system, a practical decision in some respects, but one that places a tremendous burden on astrology. It is unlikely that astrologers have ever or will ever agree upon a single worldview to complement and augment the discipline, but it is quite valuable for each of us to find some more inclusive view of existence than that offered by astrology alone.

Summary

In this chapter, we've looked at various schools of astrology, from the ancient to the modern, and have seen how they resonate with the developmental levels, culture, and esoteric/exoteric orientation we covered in previous chapters. That's a lot of ground to cover, and I have been extraordinarily brief (although the reader may feel otherwise) in my descriptions of complex material. I have also left out some approaches that are both popular and influential. Hopefully, I've established at the very least that each astrology comes from a particular developmental, cultural, and directional (inner/outer) perspective, and that these need to be taken into account when trying to understand that astrology. We can argue about the details and correct my broad generalizations in the future, but I think the basic ideas are solid.

Looking at astrology today, we can see that all of the streams that existed before the modern era have their place in the contemporary world. Instead of astrology moving ahead in a unidirectional thrust, it has flowered outwards into a plethora of schools and approaches, many of which have very little in common with each other. Rather than building on the past, astrology has resurrected traditions from all of history and across the world. Although we can question how much of ancient Mesopotamian astrology can transfer to North

America or Europe in the 21st century, it is certainly the case that some people are giving it their best shot.

Despite this expansion of astrology in many directions, we can see that some of the more prominent schools of astrology are following the path that Rudhyar foresaw as the future of astrology. Psychological astrology was one of the most popular approaches of the late 20th century, and it continues to be very prominent today. Evolutionary astrology and archetypal cosmology represent new developments that grew out of psychological astrology, and although they place their emphasis in different places, they are not inconsistent with each other.

Looking at the past is a good way to start understanding the present, and the present is the jumping-off point for the future. It appears that astrology is poised to continue its expansion throughout the developmental spectrum, speaking—in different voices—to many worldviews and perspectives.

CHAPTER 8
TOWARDS AN INTEGRAL ASTROLOGY

We've taken a look at various developmental systems, and we've related different astrologies to the developmental ladder. We also took a short tour of culture and the complexities of inner experience and outer events in the context of astrology. Then we looked at some key concepts: fate and free will, consciousness, and karma, as they relate to astrology. With this accomplished, it is time to try to map out an integral astrology, one that is capable of acknowledging both the breadth of astrology and the complexity of evolution. Such an understanding will foster compassion among diverse astrological approaches, as we begin to see the complex mosaic of astrology more clearly. I'm going to use the color-coded spectrum of Spiral Dynamics extensively, but I will also use the broader terms *preconventional*, *conventional,* and *postconventional*. After we go through the basic points of what an integral astrology might look like, the rest of the book will deal with consulting and other applications.

The following are the basic principles of an integral astrology as I see it. In time, we'll probably modify and adapt these as our understanding changes, but we must begin somewhere. Some of this material is a condensation of what was said in previous chapters, but I think it is valuable to have the ideas in a single chapter that looks forward to what astrology can become rather than an analysis of what it already is. In fact, the only real changes are not to astrology as such, but to the way we think about it.

Acknowledgement of the Development Spectrum
You can take issue with any one system, but we need to acknowledge that astrology, as a discipline that has developed over thousands of years, has traversed at least several levels of the developmental spectrum. Such an acknowledgement is necessary because an awareness that different astrologies resonate with different levels of development will help us to understand the diversity of our field, as well as to answer critics more thoughtfully. Some criticisms are only applicable to certain astrologies, for

example. That our critics tend to collapse all of astrology into a single system doesn't mean we need to do the same.

Diverse Perspectives, Diverse Astrologies

Acknowledging the developmental spectrum, the cultural foundations, and the outer and inner orientations helps us determine where any one astrology will have its usefulness. A client who is a captain of industry and very much in charge of her own ship sailing through the postconventional waters of Orange is going to be put off by a fatalistic Blue astrology reading, while a Blue client wanting to know if his ex-girlfriend will be coming back to him is likely to see a postconventional psychological astrologer as vague and unhelpful.

I am not saying, mind you, that a client who wants a fatalistic answer to what will happen necessarily ought to get one. There are too many issues—including the fallibility of astrologers—to recommend that approach. We do need to honor the client's perspective, but we also need to honor our own.

What I am saying is that each astrologer needs to understand enough about their perspective to know which clients they can serve. Giving a meaningful astrological reading is probably more dependent on the client and astrologer understanding each other's perspective (they need not necessarily share the same perspective) than on the technical skill of the astrologer.

As We Go Up the Developmental Ladder, Manifestations of Astrological Symbols Usually Become More Symbolic

This is a very important point, because so much of the criticism of astrology centers on whether astrologers can accurately predict events, describe personality traits, say what kind of career a person will have, and so on. It is also important because we need to know those same answers when working with clients. Without reference to the evolution of consciousness, we have no real way of understanding why some astrological symbols manifest as life events or in concrete ways, while others come through as internal (or psychological) processes.

Basically, the higher a person goes on the developmental spectrum, the less material an event has to be to get their attention and emotional involvement. As we move up the developmental spectrum, remember, we have greater ability to see things from multiple perspectives. Our cognitive capabilities, in terms of mental processes like logic, probably top out around the Green level, but we continue to see the world and ourselves from more inclusive perspectives as we climb the ladder of evolution. That means that as we evolve to a point somewhere between conformist Blue and achievement-oriented Orange, we start to open up the possibility of experiencing things deeply enough on the level of inner meaning that we don't *necessarily* have to have an event to make the experience real.

We can see how the process of greater symbolization works by looking at children's playthings. Early on, toddlers play with toys that look very much like the actual thing, just a bit smaller, lighter, and hopefully safer: brooms, mowers, that strangely tempting plastic food, and other almost-real stuff. A bit later on, kids like to play with things that look real, but are on a smaller scale. Consider toy cars and trucks, or the way the lifelike baby doll is replaced by the action figure. Pretty soon, although many of the earlier toys continue to hold appeal, kids can actually take an item that is merely *similar* to what they want and use their imagination to fill in the rest. I remember a yardstick that served as a sword many a time. Board games (back in the pre-video days, at least), require still more imagination: a Monopoly board doesn't really look much like Atlantic City, and Risk is a very abstract way to take over the world. We can see how children's toys and games become progressively more symbolic as they grow and their cognitive capabilities increase.

In a similar way, astrological symbols, both natal and by transit, can become less concrete in their manifestation as we evolve. This doesn't mean events can't happen to people at higher levels, but it does mean that people at the lower developmental levels cannot experience the symbol without some concrete event. As we get higher on the evolutionary spectrum, we can *imagine* our way through more of life, and have less of a need to *act out* our lessons.

Astrological Symbols Are Multivalent, and Can Manifest at Any Level Up to and Including the Person's Highest Developmental Level

That's a mouthful, but it should be obvious. A given astrological symbol, say transiting Pluto opposing natal Saturn, can manifest in a variety of ways. For a person at the Blue, conventional level, that might mean losing their job, taking a pay cut, and so on. For a person a couple of levels above at postconventional Green, it could manifest as a deep questioning of the value of the work they are doing and a crisis of meaning in their career. The person at Green *could* also lose her job, of course. But the person at Blue *cannot* have a crisis of meaning in his career—that just isn't a possibility as long as he remains at Blue.[1]

At each level, the symbol can and usually does manifest in a variety of ways, although clients and astrologers often focus on a single important facet. So, a woman who has a Uranus transit to her natal Venus may find that she is attracted to a new type of person. She might also find that she is attracted to people who are somewhat aloof and Uranian by nature (maybe Aquarians start looking especially hot). And she herself might become somewhat more aloof and independent in her attitude towards relationship. Her aesthetic sense may change, also, and that change could very well be towards artwork with a political message. And so on. We'll cover this idea in more depth in the next chapter, on fractals and attractors. For now, the point is that multiple meanings tend to emerge out of the same symbol, and they do so at levels up to and including the person's highest developmental level.

The astrological chart itself only describes the conditions that will turn up on each developmental level. That is, as we get on top of issues at one level, we move up to a new developmental stage, where those issues recreate themselves at a higher level.

The Manifestation of an Astrological Symbol on the Person's Highest Developmental Level Will Be Felt Most Acutely

Usually, at any rate.

Returning to the example of Pluto transiting Saturn, a person at the postconventional Green level who goes through a crisis of meaning in her career and has to find a new direction feels that crisis just as intensely as the person at conventional Blue who gets laid off. Now, there are of course caveats, and I don't want to sound glib. But as hard is it may be for a person at Blue to fathom, people at Green suffer just as much when they drag themselves to jobs that go against their values (or seems valueless) as that person at Blue feels when the pink slip arrives. The person at Green will not feel the pain of getting laid off as strongly as the person at Blue, however. If you tell this to a person at conventional Blue, they will roll their eyes and think you are talking mumbo-jumbo, and that you have no idea how bad it is to get laid off.

"So what if you don't like your work, at least you still have a job!" they'll say. And from their perspective, they are right. But for the person at the postconventional level who needs to feel that they are contributing to a good cause, they may very well prove how much it means to them—by quitting their job.

Astrology Can Predict Opportunities for Consciousness Evolution, but Not Whether It Will Occur

To put it another way, astrology describes the conditions that obtain at any developmental level, but does not and cannot say anything about an individual's developmental level per se. That includes transitions from one level to the next. When we see a transit coming, we might suspect that it is sufficiently stressful to move a person from one level to another. For example, we might reason that the Pluto transit to Saturn could put enough stress on a person at the conventional Blue level to see past the limitations of his job situation and develop a more postconventional game-player type of approach.

And it might. But we don't know through astrology whether that will be the case. Even when we take into account the house positions and rulerships and signs and so on, we still won't know for sure. After all, we also don't know through astrology what developmental level the person is on at this point, and we don't know how they have handled past transits that might have provided similar impetus for growth.

The natal chart surely cannot help. After all, you can't look at a natal chart and estimate developmental level, since the chart remains the same throughout life. We can't say, "This is the chart of a postconventional person," because it is the same chart that the person had when they were two years old, and no two-year-old is postconventional. Yes, there are progressions to the natal chart, but as with the natal chart and transits, they open up possibilities rather than describing outcomes.

Astrologers generally know this, although we might not formulate it in these terms. If you look at the chart of someone who has a hard natal aspect of Saturn to the sun, for example, you know what kind of issues the person will have with authority figures, self-esteem, and so on. But we also recognize that while this is a challenging aspect, an individual who accepts the challenge and works at it can accomplish a great deal. We sometimes speak of better and worse or higher and lower manifestations of such an aspect. In other words, the person has either used the aspect for development, or has allowed it to rule their life. Until we talk to the client, though, we just don't know.

Astrology does not measure awareness, the basic quality of consciousness. Astrology can describe conditions that might tend towards increasing awareness, but the process of letting go of one's current evolutionary level in favor of a new one is not a process that is adequately described astrologically. For that, one has to turn to the developmental literature.

Any Astrology Should Be Assessed in Terms Relevant to Its Perspective

Let's look at how we assess the validity of astrology. To date, very few astrologers have tackled this issue, and credit has to be given to anyone who has found the time and energy to deal with this topic. This is an expansion of the ideas I brought up when talking about scientific astrology, but it is relevant not only to trying to measure astrological variables scientifically but also to assessing any astrology's validity.

Assessing the validity of *astrology* as a whole is impossible, because as we know, there isn't one astrology, there are many *astrologies*. Each astrology has its own perspective, and it needs to be assessed in ways that are appropriate to that perspective. If event-orient Uranian or scientific astrologers maintain that they can predict concrete events in peoples' lives, then we can make some attempt to measure their accuracy using the sort of scientific techniques we would use to measure the accuracy of weather predictions. That is *appropriate* for those kinds of event-oriented astrologies (although not necessarily all event-oriented astrologies).

It is not, however, appropriate for psychological or evolutionary astrology. Those approaches would have to be measured in a different way, for example through narrative analysis and comparison, or by talking to clients to discover how they feel before and after a reading. There are many good techniques out there for working with meaning and feelings, but they aren't the same kind of techniques that are used for measuring the physical world. Qualitative research has proved much more helpful than quantitative statistical analysis when it comes to understanding various social trends, for example. Hermeneutics is a way to assess shared experience, and the techniques of phenomenology can serve as tools for elucidating individual experience. I am not going to try to match up investigative techniques to astrologies, because interested researchers should be able to do it themselves and because there are many techniques that would be valid for any astrology. But recognize that there are many astrologies, and find a technique that is appropriate to assess the one at which you are looking.

An Astrology Will Work Best on Its Own Level

Astrologers sometimes look back with nostalgia at the "good old days," when William Lilly could predict the great London fire, and other marvelous predictions were made. Of course, like fishing tales, we get to hear the successes more than the failures, but certainly concrete predictive astrology had its glory days.

But that was then. In a conventional society, concrete predictions are far more likely to be successful than in a postconventional society, because in the conventional culture limited outcomes are possible and the potential for symbolic variability has not yet fully emerged.

Conventional astrology works well for conventional society. In a postconventional society, a postconventional astrology will work much better. If Liz Greene had started talking to Londoners in the 15th century, she wouldn't have made any sense with her postconventional, psychological astrology. An astrology situated at a given developmental level will not be *intelligible* to lower levels, and will not be *effective* for higher ones.

Astrology Is Not, and Never Has Been, A Free-for-All

I'm going to answer two important criticisms here. The first is that astrology is not a science, and so is pervaded by sloppy thinking and pseudoscientific claims. The second is that by advocating for multiple perspectives and the validity of each, I am essentially saying that anything goes, or: as long as you believe in it, it works.

Astrology is not a science, at least in the currently accepted meaning of the word. It never has been, and astrologers ought to let go of the claim that it is. But that doesn't mean that astrology is merely a hodge-podge of ideas that anyone can add to without critical review. Astrologers, like members of any discipline, will select new ideas and work with them, test them out, and eventually accept or discard them. Astrologers will look to see if an idea is a challenge to the self-consistency of their system, and they will assess its utility in a variety of contexts. It is a less precise kind of trial and error process than that which occurs in the scientific community, but is by no means arbitrary. Just as fish and chips is likely to be rejected as French cuisine, so astrology is capable of vetting new ideas without being scientific. We are just as capable of sorting out our ideas as any other discipline. If academia is going to be our standard, a good practice might be to look to the humanities, rather than the sciences, for models.[2]

When I say that each astrology is valid from its own perspective, I am not saying that astrology is entirely subjective, without reference to anything external to our constructed meanings. I *am* saying that no astrology can exist without being embedded in our constructed meanings, and the best way to understand those meanings is to look at the developmental level, culture, and inner/outer perspective they represent. That won't tell you everything about an astrology, but it will tell you a great deal.

Astrology does sit in an uncomfortable place. It doesn't belong among the physical sciences because it is so dependent on meaning and symbols, but it does relate in a direct way to physical phenomena. Everything relates to everything, of course, if you think about it. Art and literature have a physical dimension, as is apparent when we consider the materials used and the media through which they are displayed. But astrology is different. If Uranus is moving into tropical Aries, tropical astrologers who use the outer planets ought to be able to notice something significant at some level. And there ought to be at least some consistency, some symbolic harmony, despite the perspectives of the astrologers and their schools.

As I have said, even without scientific method I believe we have such consistency. Because we come from different perspectives that reflect different levels of development and different orientations, it can be hard to see that when we look at astrology across the board, but it is there. I know of no astrology, for example, that sees Mars as a warm and fuzzy planet (warm, maybe—but not fuzzy). Saturn isn't a load of fun in any system, Eastern or Western. And Jupiter and Venus get good press in every system I have seen. There may be exceptions, but they are rare and have not pushed their way into our contemporary consciousness—at a time when any system from any era has a shot at the big time via the Internet.

So, no, astrology is not a free-for-all. It is not a science, and it does have a great deal of variety, with more to come. But there are a few aspects of astrology that are consistent regardless of era or place, and much of the variation can be explained by either the evolutionary process, culture, or the inner/outer orientation. Astrology is neither a given, out there to be discovered, nor is it strictly imaginal. Rather, astrologies are constructed by an interaction of our evolving understanding with a dynamic, changing universe.

Astrological Symbols Are Evolutionary

Throughout this book so far, I have been emphasizing the process of development—evolution of consciousness—in human terms. That's important for understanding how different astrologies are created and applied, but evolution is not strictly anthropocentric.

When we talk about evolution, we are often talking about the biological evolution of species of plants and animals on the Earth. From a larger perspective, we can include the entire process of creation in the Universe, starting with the Big Bang (or whatever you like), and moving through levels of energy into matter, then matter into life, life into consciousness, and then ever-increasing and more inclusive levels of consciousness. From this larger perspective, humans aren't the pinnacle of evolution (although we're doing fairly well), but are manifestations of something that transcends any one of its particular manifestations, humans included.

When we operate with this larger understanding, we see that the entire cosmos is in a process of evolution, becoming ever more conscious of itself. So, as we move up the evolutionary ladder and create astrologies that reflect these higher developmental levels, we aren't simply reading something we couldn't read before, we are co-creating the higher, symbolic meanings *with* the Universe. Again, it is neither all subjective, nor is there an objective truth that is simply waiting to be discovered.

Pluto can serve as an example. Until 1931, no one knew the Pluto existed, and astrology up to that point in time was getting along fairly well in its pre-Plutonian way. Then, when Pluto was discovered and named, we set to work on creating the astrological meanings associated with the planet, and these have changed and deepened over time. Astronomers get to name the planets, but they seem to do a remarkable job of allowing synchronicity to work in the process.

Now, the question comes up, was Pluto active before we found it? Well, if we go back into time and look various transits and sign changes, we would probably say that it was. Richard Tarnas has done an excellent job of doing exactly that, as a good deal of *Cosmos and Psyche* is about the transits of the three outer planets before they were discovered. Like gravity before Newton, it seems that there was something active, even if we couldn't describe it accurately or recognize it. But how could there be *meaningful* effects without someone to see the meaning? Can meaning exist apart from the human mind?

Recall that Boethius said *knowledge is a product of the knower, not the object.* It is not that people in the 14th century were walking around under the influence of Neptune and Pluto but didn't know it. The astrology of the day would have explained everything that was going on perfectly adequately. Our post-Uranian explanations would and could only make sense in a post-Uranian world. To put it another way, Tarnas' *Cosmos and Psyche* would have made little sense to a 14th century astrologer, even if you explained to him about the newer planets. Consider that before the 18th century, the word *revolution* did not exist in a political context, but meant simply *to revolve*, like a wheel, then decide how you would explain the planet Uranus.[3] Whether there is a consciousness apart from human consciousness that would have understood the symbolic meaning of the outer planets is a separate (and interesting) question, but I am inclined to think that astrology is very much tied to the human perspective, and would have less relevance for an angel, an extraterrestrial, or others.

So, just as humans evolve, and just as consciousness in the Universe evolves, so astrology also evolves. Astrological meanings are neither waiting out there to be discovered (inherent in a planet, house system, sign, or aspect), nor are they created out of an astrologer's whim. Rather, as consciousness evolves, the symbolic meaning of astrological symbols also evolves. Consider how Mars went from being strictly malefic and associated with wars and aggression, to being understood as important in terms of assertiveness. As people have become better at understanding their own motivations, energies symbolized by the planets have come under greater conscious control, and even difficult energies such as those of Mars and Saturn are understood to have potentially constructive functions, *even when placed in difficult positions.*[4]

Not only are astrological symbols multivalent, capable of manifesting in various ways at multiple levels of development, and not only will particular circumstances endlessly create myriad possibilities; as we continue to evolve there will continue to be higher and higher levels of manifestation of each symbol.

Astrology Is Just Astrology

I said it in the introduction, but I will repeat it here because it very important: astrology is not a *theory of everything*. Astrology, like many disciplines, can look at just about anything, taking it as an object of inquiry. That doesn't mean, though, that astrology is a grand scheme that takes all perspectives into account. When astrologers look at an individual, the history of a nation, global economics, scientific discoveries, and other things, we are looking at them through the lens of astrology. That we can learn a great deal about these things and ourselves in the process is of course true (at least for most people reading this book), but that is very different from actually knowing about the thing from various other perspectives inside and outside of it. One might be able to predict changes in the stock market using astrology, but that is different from knowledge of economics.[5]

Inner and Outer Reflect Each Other

Throughout this book, and throughout anyone's study of astrology, there are a number of instances of the dichotomy between inner and outer experience. We discussed it in reference to the source of change: when does change come from within, and when does it come from without? We also talked about it when discussing the orientation of astrologies: some focus on our inner experience, some focus on events in the physical world. We even touched on this topic when talking about the value memes and developmental level (at least we did if you're reading the notes), because some levels and memes are inner-directed and some are outer-directed.

Yet despite the obvious value in simplifying things this way—and I advocated for such simplification in a previous chapter—we have to remember that the real situation is far more complex than a basic *either/or* dichotomy. For example, change that comes from within a person may be precipitated by external events (even those in the distant past), and change that seems to befall a person from without (like getting fired) might be precipitated by an inner change (really disliking one's job). Not that we want to take things so far as to "blame the victim" when truly horrific things like illness, wars, and crimes take place, but many of life's external struggles are mirrors of internal states, and vice-versa.

We need to be mindful of the inner/outer distinction and account for it, but on the other hand we ought not to get too caught up in it. Few astrologers today, and even in the past, believe that the stars *impel* so much as *signify*, so we don't need to focus on causality. We are looking at symbolic meaning, and that will have both inner and outer dimensions. The reciprocal nature of inner experience and outer events means that any truly integral astrology will have to account for both. Purely psychological or purely event-oriented astrologies have their values, but those values are only partial. When it comes to the inner/outer distinction, we should recognize the difference in the perspectives and our own bias towards one of them, but our astrology should strive to be *both/and* rather than *either/or*.

The Astrologer Is in a Learning Process, Just as the Client Is

If you give professionals in prestigious occupations the chance to fill out an anonymous questionnaire, you often get some surprising results. Among them is that many top-of-the-line professionals in top-of-the-line professions feel somewhat insecure about their professional abilities. I worked in health care for a long time, and it always seemed to me that the bluster of some doctors was based on an inner insecurity: they pulled rank so they wouldn't have to argue their position. If insecurity is found in high-prestige professions, we might expect it to have at least equal representation among astrologers.

Then there is the professional stance: Me professional, you client. That separation, and the hierarchy it creates, is part and parcel of the way most professions operate. At least in the matter at hand, the professional is the expert and the client is a more or less passive recipient, and often in a position of dependence. If there is insecurity on the part of the professional, this stance is often invoked and exaggerated so that the professional can be both apart from and above the client. Professional *stance* becomes professional *distance*. For example, professional terminology is fine (it can help clients to label and so contain things they might otherwise have difficulty understanding, while also showing the professional is not just making things up), but the descent into jargon and mumbo-jumbo is a marker for insecurities and overreliance on professional distance.

These professional issues become much less problematic when we take the bold but realistic step of accepting that we don't know everything. Many astrologers recognize in themselves a desire to help their clients, and perhaps to further the client's growth and development. That's wonderful, and it shows astrology to be a service profession, rather than the entertainment or fortune telling it is often assumed to be. Yet the astrologer also needs to acknowledge that they themselves are in the process of growing and developing, professionally and otherwise.

When we open up to the possibility that each client can teach us something new and broaden our understanding of astrology (and other things), we also open up to the possibility of our own growth and development. Not only can we accrue more technical information about astrology, we can also see the many ways symbols manifest at different levels and from a variety of perspectives. Readings can become more flexible and open, a creative dialogue between the astrologer and the client. The astrologer brings a wealth of astrological knowledge, and the client brings the particulars. Together, they create a meaningful interpretation that weaves the two together. At the end of the consultation, *everyone* has learned something.

We also need to have a degree of humility when we reflect on ourselves outside of the consultation room. It's easy to say that I am a better astrologer now than I was ten years ago. It's a little harder to say that I am a better astrologer than I was one year ago, because that is close enough in time that part of me feels I should have already been as good last year as I am this year. Then there's next year, when I will hopefully be an even better astrologer. Obviously, the positive side is that I can grow and become more competent and be of greater service to my clients. Yet it also means that I am not "the best" astrologer today, and also that *I don't yet know* what will make me a better astrologer in the future. That not-knowing can be a hard pill for any professional to swallow. We have to work our way into the future with all kinds of learning experiences, some of them difficult. That means accepting that no matter how competent we are now, in a sense we are still students.

The Form of the Astrological Practice Should Reflect Its Approach

There is very little written about the actual practice of astrology as a business. The few books I've found and read on the subject, by Stephen Arroyo, Robert Blaschke, and Donna Cunningham, are all excellent sources: I would just note that they are written from the postconventional, humanistic, perspective of psychological astrology.

How each astrologer approaches the business side of their practice varies a great deal. I worked as a speech pathologist for a number of years, and I approached my practice essentially with the *professional* model, very similar to Blaschke, Cunningham, and Arroyo. Other astrologers come from the *business* world, and take that approach into astrology, selling a variety of products and services and using business-like marketing strategies. Still others approach from a more New Age angle, and let their practice build itself. Most of us, myself included, actually blend these and other approaches, although one may predominate.

What matters is that the practice should reflect the astrological approach. When it comes to advertising and other marketing strategies, some of the best ideas only work well if you want to do a particular kind of work. A particular strategy might bring in a lot of clients, but you have to consider whether they are going to want the services you offer. I have no real interest in helping people to pick good times to gamble, for example, and I'm not much of a medical astrologer, either. There's nothing wrong with those applications of astrology for those who are interested, as should be obvious from my assertion that the astrology, the astrologer, and the client all have to match up. But my point is that marketing strategies might wind up encouraging clients with issues you really don't want to deal with, and probably would not be great at addressing. An astrologer who wants to work with business clients might get frustrated by the responses she gets to ads in a New Age magazine. You get the idea.

Summary

If we want others to recognize astrology—or even to criticize it more realistically—and if we want to understand our own discipline, we need a framework that connects our thinking to the rest of the world. I believe the integral astrology I have outlined offers that.

In a nutshell, traditional astrologers (William Lilly, Ptolemy) assumed astrology was valid from within from within their cultural matrix; modern astrologers assumed that we would develop an astrology that superseded cultural limitations; postmodern astrologers advocated for the inclusion of multiple astrologies simultaneously, with respect for each cultural matrix; and integral astrology acknowledges the various astrologies but also orders them hierarchically and according to their perspective so that their value and relevance can be applied optimally.

Astrologers generally respect each other's differences. We're far more cordial than many disciplines that are divided by ideological differences. Where we have been less successful is in recognizing the origins of those differences, and how they can be reconciled into a larger whole that acknowledges the value of each perspective, not just out of cordiality, but out of an overarching and inclusive understanding.

CHAPTER 9
FRACTALS AND ATTRACTORS

In this chapter, I want to introduce a couple of concepts from chaos theory, one of the New Paradigm sciences. In terms of astrology, I believe this represents a slightly different way of thinking about symbols, a new metaphor. The real value is in demonstrating how astrology can change its language in such a way that will make it more accessible to other disciplines. I don't think that we ought to lose any of our existing terminology, some of which is thousands of years old and rich with centuries of meaning, but we can also explore ways that will help us relate to contemporary thinking, while demonstrating some similarities between astrology and other disciplines.

I am generally not a fan of most of the grafting of New Paradigm science onto New Age ideas. I roll my eyes when I hear people talking about how quantum physicists have proven that we have free will or that consciousness exists.[1] For one thing, few New Agers have taken the time to learn the physics involved, and most of what we get are extremely watered-down versions, usually in the form of some cute little story, like Schrödinger's Cat. Basing spiritual truth on physical cosmology is highly problematic even when you understand it, and it's exactly what caused the Catholic Church so much trouble when Copernicus upended the geocentric model of the universe.[2]

Some *parallels* between the physical and metaphysical do run through existence, but they are not *identical* on every level of being. Things get more complex as we move up the evolutionary ladder, for example. What is true of matter might in some way resonate with mind and soul, but psychology and geology are different sciences because they look at different levels of organization. Scientific understanding of matter, energy, and other physical properties is still the mental level understanding the physical, not the physical level in itself. It is important to be very, very careful in attemping to base a metaphysics on physics.

Before I go on, I ought to make one point clear. Fractals and attractors are mathematical, scientific concepts that have rather specific meanings. I might be in danger of doing exactly what I have cautioned against—that is, borrowing an idea from one area and applying it to another without considering the leap in levels of existence. But I will press ahead, because fractals and attractors are applicable to multiple levels of reality, as theorists find new ways to be flexible with their definitions. As you will see, such flexibility seems logically consistent with the concepts themselves. At worst I am using fractals and attractors as analogies, and I am ready to accept the limitations that go with that.

Chaos and its cousin complexity are two new branches of science that aren't rooted in any one particular level of existence, but rather in understanding the patterns that emerge at each level. Given that, it is possible to see how similar patterns often emerge at diverse levels. It seems to suggest that there are some basic patterns that keep emerging all over the cosmic landscape, the way galaxies and the soap suds in your sink both form spirals. That should sound very familiar to astrologers, because it is another way of saying "as above, so below."

There are two significant differences with this approach in comparison to the simple grafting of one level of understanding onto another. The first is that the comparison of patterns comes from empirical data. We can look at physical processes in nature like whirlpools and spiral galaxies, and also at snail shells and other things, and note the similarities. That's very different from saying that because electrons behave a certain way, we must have free will. Noting similarities is not the same as making an assertion about one level of reality based on what you see at another. The second is that similarities at different levels of reality don't imply any causal relationship, at least not between those two levels (although logically a third party could be causing the similarities at each level). When people start talking about a quantum field that contains all information in the cosmos, they are making meaningful reality dependent on physical reality. If all we do is note that information is found all over the cosmos, it is a subtly different statement. Fortunately, the two ideas that I want to bring into astrology are relatively free from this baggage.

Fractals

A fractal is a self-similar shape that reproduces itself at multiple levels. If you want to get even more technical, it is impossible (or at least very difficult) to determine the level of scale without an external reference. That sounds very complicated, but fractals are all around us. A simple way to think about fractals is to recognize that frequently the parts of a thing will resemble the whole.

Think about a tree. A nice, ordinary maple or oak should do nicely. Imagine the basic structure of the tree, with its trunk, larger branches on the bottom tapering to smaller branches on the top. Now, imagine that we go about half way up through the canopy of the tree and saw off one of the branches coming out of the trunk. We then plant it next to the tree from which it came. It looks very much like a smaller version of the original tree. Now let's go about half way up this branch and select a branch that is coming off of this smaller tree. We saw it off and plant it in the ground, and lo and behold, it also looks like a smaller version of the original tree. Go about halfway up this mini-tree, clip off a large twig and plant it in the ground, and we have a smaller mini-tree again. Clip a small twig off of this and put it into a model railroad, and you have a nice frame for a two- or three-inch tree. The branch structure of most trees is self-similar at every level.

As another example, look at a fern leaf. The overall shape of the leaf is repeated in each of the leaflets, and even the smaller lobes that form the leaflets have a similar overall shape.

Maps offer another opportunity to see how patterns can resemble each other at multiple levels of scale. If you look at a map—say a section of coastline—and you don't know the scale, you have no idea what you're looking at. On a map, an island will look about the same whether it is one, ten, or fifty miles in diameter. You can get the same effect flying over mountains or waves in an airplane. It is impossible to estimate their size until you see a car, a boat, or some other object to serve as a point of reference, because mountains and waves are self-similar at every level of scale.

While nature offers amazing evidence of fractals, humans construct some very fractal-like things, as well. A modern city like New York is usually laid out on a grid pattern, with regular rectangular blocks. If we look at each of those blocks, we see that they are divided into rectangular lots, on which rectangular buildings are constructed. Look at the plan of each building, and you'll notice it is subdivided into rectangular suites—offices or apartments—that are further subdivided into rectangular rooms. Even taking into account the round potted plant and the curve of the chair, we can see that much of the furniture in the room, like tables, wall units, dressers, and divans, are also rectangular in shape, and some of *them* are even subdivided into rectangular drawers. Midtown Manhattan is truly a study in rectangles!

Computer-generated fractal images are beautiful and often have an uncanny resemblance to natural landscapes. They are created by feeding the results of a mathematical equation back into itself, in an ongoing loop. Feedback loops are easy enough to understand mathematically. For example, we can take a very simple term, like $x+2=y$, and start off with $x=1$. The resulting answer is 3, and we make the new x equal to three, so that y becomes 5, and then 5 becomes the new x, and so on. That equation won't make a fractal, in fact it will only make a line with a shallow slope. Actual fractal equations aren't necessarily very complicated, although computers are needed to do the work of plotting out the complex curves through many millions of points.

What does this have to do with astrology? Well, remember that astrological symbols are multivalent and that they will manifest as both inner experience and outer events on all levels up to the individual's (or group's) highest developmental level, and that there will usually be more than one exemplar on each level. That sounds remarkably like a fractal, doesn't it?

Astrologers spend a lot of energy trying to pin down how a particular symbol is going to appear. That's true of natal astrology, when we look to see what kind of career or partner a person might have, and it is especially true of transits and progressions. If we use fractals as our model, we can see that there will be many manifestations, all of them self-similar in meaning yet different in scale (developmental level and importance to the person) and exhibiting slight variations. The example I gave earlier about a woman having a Uranus transit to her Venus is an example of the fractal nature of the transit—it manifests in many ways at multiple levels.

The basic aspect under consideration is a bit like the fractal equation: not very complicated in itself, although when we're dealing with meaning it's never going to be as clear cut as plotting numbers. An astrologer ought to have a pretty good and relatively simple idea of what Jupiter square Mercury means in the natal chart, for example. Right away, we can take the cookbook keywords and come up with a basic definition. Most astrologers will fill out the equation with things like sign and house placements, rulerships, dignities and debilities. Astrologers who are interested in mythology can start thinking about stories from mythology involving these two gods, perhaps even moving across cultures. Uranian astrologers can look up the explanation of how these two planets influence each other. One way or another, we come up with a basic blueprint, an equation that represents this aspect.

Because we can describe astrological meaning as fractal, that Jupiter square to Mercury is going to color thought and communication in many ways. How the person handles each manifestation of it—on an ongoing basis—will affect the way the next situation arises, and so on. The aspect is always there, generating opportunities to work with it more or less consciously. It is like the result of one equation feeding back into the next iteration of the equation, but with the difference that awareness is an additional factor that you can't know, because it varies.

The current manifestation of a natal aspect will be influenced not only by the planets and other astrological factors, but also by how the person has handled every other manifestation of that aspect, as well as their level of awareness of the energies involved. The equation becomes $(Jupiter\ square\ Mercury)_{history}$ x $Awareness =$ $(Jupiter\ square\ Mercury)_{now}$. Increase the awareness and you can get a whole new level of possibilities for the aspect, similar in some ways to the previous manifestations, but with differences in scale. Keywords and definitions are good, but we need to recognize that the inner meaning of the aspect can generate infinite possibilities for surface manifestations. Astrology sets parameters and determines the basic form, but can't account for awareness or history. Like an oak tree, an astrological factor will have a recognizable form, but also like oaks there will be variations from tree to tree and on the branches within trees.

If the level of awareness remains low, there will be very little inclination to change the overall pattern of a natal aspect, and so the current iteration will more or less resemble the last. Over time, the natal aspect can become concretized into an entrenched personality trait. In our Jupiter/Mercury example, we get bombastic Uncle Dave, who is always ready to espouse his opinions about everything to anyone he can corner at the family reunion. Astrological aspects don't create personality traits, however, they only lay out a field of energetic patterns, with infinite potential variations. Personality characteristics are the result of an ongoing repetition of the same choice within that field of potential. Traditional astrology textbooks could assert that an aspect (or any other astrological factor) would correlate to a character trait because they were comfortable in assuming a level of awareness (conventional or below) where they expected very little variation in the way an aspect would manifest.

Transits show similar potentials, although condensed in time. During the months or years a transit is in effect, the person's life will become colored by its ongoing appearance in many forms. Given that a transit will manifest on any and all levels up to a person's highest level of awareness, the big event associated with a transit might be seen as the manifestation that really catches their awareness and holds the potential for them to work with the energies in a conscious way. From that perspective, Aunt Flora's Jupiter/Mercury transit isn't about her buying a big car, buying a big car is what calls attention to her Jupiter/Mercury transit.

The manifestations of a natal aspect or a transit will occur within a person, and in their life as we view it from without. It will also characterize many aspects of their relationships with others, and will probably be found in the charts of those with whom they have relationships. In the example I gave earlier, a woman with transiting Uranus aspecting her Venus may seek a new relationship, with a Uranian type of person, and that relationship may be characterized by a great deal of freedom. At the same time, her image of what an ideal woman is may change, and in such a way that highlights Uranian or Aquarian values. Her sense of aesthetics may change as well. Inside and outside, and at all levels, the basic energy of the transit manifests in a fractal-like pattern.[3]

Attractors

Astrology's roots extend back into the mythic era, a time when myth communicated meaning through a symbol system that was largely unconscious. That it was not a fully conscious system is apparent when we consider that most people at that time were not yet fully differentiated individuals. Early in the mythic period, most people were at the preconventional Purple level, where there is not a complete isolation of the ego.

Myth is still around us, of course, and we participate in creating and digesting it both consciously (*Star Wars*) and with less consciousness (professional wrestling). Like everything else, myth has evolved, and the meanings of myth (even very ancient ones) have taken on more highly evolved and complex meanings over time. I question the extent to which a person who is at a postconventional level can truly participate in mythic consciousness, because part of us is always analyzing and decoding the meanings, but myth is certainly still an active force.

Myth is also a valuable facet of astrology. We can use references to myths to illuminate an astrological condition, and we can create our own myths (or, less grandly, *stories*) to explain astrological meaning. We might reference recent history, for example, or use a movie to explain a transit. In my book *Transformation*, I listed movies, songs, and books that resonate with particular transits. These can be considered modern myths, stories that we create to demonstrate truths about our psyches and the world. This process seems to be ongoing on a collective level in the naming of planets, planetoids, and asteroids. For example, we've broken out of the mold that had everything named for Roman gods and goddesses, and now have asteroids named for Egyptian deities, like Isis, and even for contemporary figures like *Monty Python*.

Jung's *archetypes* are another model for describing astrological symbols. An archetype is a basic pattern that has essentially infinite variety of expression. For example, we can see the *mother* archetype as manifesting in the Virgin Mary, the goddess Demeter, Kwan Yin, the collegiate *alma mater*,[4] Mother Earth, Gaia, and in many other places. Each of these specific manifestations has its own variations on the theme of mother, but each is clearly distinct from the *warrior* archetype. Over the course of his long career, Jung's view of archetypes developed considerably. Initially, he related the variety of images we find constellating around a theme as reflecting biological structures in the brain, but in his later writings he speculated that they also had a spiritual (that is, metaphysical) dimension.

Archetypes are frequently invoked to describe astrological symbols, and it should be obvious that they have a great deal in common, as do all true symbols. In fact, when we consider the *moon* and the *mother* archetype, or *Mars* and the *warrior*, we are really speaking about the same thing, although from an astrological and a mythic/psychological perspective they have different names and different applications.

We can broaden our understanding of astrological symbols and archetypes with an idea from chaos theory, the notion of a *strange attractor*. An attractor is a pattern that characterizes the movement of a system. This pattern is essentially self-maintaining. There are a variety of types of attractors, from static attractors that represent a system coming to rest (like water forming a puddle) to periodic attractors that describe regular motion (like the seasons of the year) to strange attractors that describe a regular pattern that has variable manifestations. The pattern of a strange attractor may only become apparent over a long course of many trials or cycles, and even then the next movement of the system will not be precisely predictable.

Science has traditionally stressed a cause and effect relationship between factors, with the aim of predicting activity as precisely as possible. The problem is that as systems become more complex, it is more and more difficult to account for the multitude of factors that come into play. It is not the case that an intelligible pattern is not present, but rather that it is the general pattern that is reliable, not any one specific data point. The underlying pattern informs the system in a way that is not always apparent from looking at the surface manifestations. Many natural attractor patterns have to be graphed out to become apparent, for example, and so fall into the category of strange attractors.

We can take the weather as an example. Weather is a very complex phenomenon, dependent partially on the periodic attractor of the seasons, but in itself it represents a strange attractor. Hurricane season in the Atlantic Ocean stretches roughly from June to November. It is during those months that hurricanes are most likely to develop, and each year residents of the Caribbean region keep a nervous eye on the tropical depressions that start off the coast of Africa. But although we know when the overall conditions for hurricanes are most likely to develop, we don't know anything about what the tropical storm situation will be on any given September 1st. Some years, there are many hurricanes, some years there are very few. Some years, there are strong category 4 storms, some years there are none. Each storm may track northwards to hit the east coast of the United States, or go on a more southerly course towards the Gulf of Mexico. Although at every level the pattern is recognizable, at no point is it entirely predictable.[5]

This example of weather patterns, although simple and a bit problematic, should give you the basic idea of how a strange attractor works. You can recognize an underlying pattern, but you can't be exactly sure where things are going next. You also have to observe the pattern over time to see how it is manifesting, or in fact to see it at all. If we were to fly you to some undetermined part of the earth and plunk you down without any hint as to where you were, you'd have to watch the weather for a long time—at least a year—to have an idea of the pattern.

Strange attractors are all over the place. Economists talk about the business cycle, a discernible pattern that has a lot of variation. Even the value memes that describe the various stages of development can be thought of as strange attractors. After all, we know someone at postconventional Orange will be inclined to rely on their own judgment, and to use a left-brain kind of approach to life. But we don't know if that person will go into business, a university, or some other way of expressing Orange values. In fact, one of the facets of postconventional reality is the ability to create infinite possibilities—although there is still plenty of variation at the preconventional and conventional levels.

The idea of an underlying pattern that manifests with greater predictability when we look at it over time but with less specificity at any one point in time should have obvious value for astrologers, as this is exactly what astrological factors do. We know a lot about Jupiter, for instance, but what we know with the most certainty is rather general. How Jupiter will be active today, in my chart, your chart, in mundane astrology, and so on, is far less certain.

Let's look at it this way: we know Jupiter, and we know Mars. These two symbols are sufficiently distinct from one another that even the most casual student of astrology would be able to differentiate the associated activity of one from the other. If I tell you that my car was hit on the day that one of these planets went over my ascendant a few years ago, and that I recently received a very positive email from a university professor, you will have no problem matching the planets to their respective events. In this simple example of matching manifestation to symbol we can recognize the pattern of each planet with relative ease.

On the other hand, when it comes to generating possibilities for how a symbol will appear, the best we can do is to describe the overall pattern, with little detail. If I tell you that I recently had a Neptune transit to my IC (opposite my midheaven), you will have a much more difficult time describing what happened, compared to matching the energies of Jupiter and Mars to the events associated with their transits. Yes, if you had my full chart in front of you, you could narrow things down or generate more meaningful alternatives. You will almost *certainly* be correct about the general flavor of the transit, but at a loss for details. As we fill in the chart details, it is like focusing on a summer or winter month—we can narrow the parameters of the transit. But the specifics are still like using our knowledge of hurricane season to predict the weather on a single day.

When we look at astrological factors as attractors, and strange ones at that, we recognize at once that there are reliable patterns of meaning associated them, but not specific definitions. There are at least two reasons for this. Because astrological symbols are in fact *symbols* and not *signs*, they are generative, like archetypes, and can and will always find new ways to crop up in the world. Mars and Jupiter aren't going to be confused with each other any more than summer and winter, but like *this* summer and *this* winter, they will manifest in unique ways. That becomes more apparent in light of the other factor, interaction. We never really get to see astrological factors in isolation. You can never look only at Venus, for example. Even if she is unaspected, she will be in a sign, rising in the morning or setting in the evening, and so on. There is no way to isolate an astrological factor and take it into the lab and see what it does all by itself. Again, this is very much like the weather, where any one factor (like humidity) can only be seen within the context of all the other meteorological factors operating at the same time. That doesn't stop us from seeing a reliable pattern, but it does make it very hard to see specifics.

As an example of how astrological symbols can be seen as attractors, let's look at a hard transit of Saturn to a man's Mars. We could use a natal aspect, too, but I think a transit might be easier to see. First, let us assume that the man is in something like a steady state: there are no other major transits taking place at the same time as this one. Let's remember, though, that a living human—or an active anything—is never really in a steady state. We can be in *balance*, but that doesn't mean nothing is going on. In other words, even when we feel ourselves to be in a more or less steady state, it isn't like we are rocks sitting on the ground, not moving at all. It is more like we are driving down a stretch of highway. There's not a lot to do, but you have to keep alert, make minor steering and acceleration corrections, and so on. Among other things, you'll be consuming energy.

Okay, though, our example man is in a relatively steady state. His natal chart is buzzing and humming as always, but there are no transits going on. As Saturn starts to move in on his Mars, however, he begins to feel a pull on his energy. This will begin to happen when Saturn is still quite far off, perhaps as soon as Saturn enters the relevant sign. At first, the differences are very subtle, as he hovers around the edge of the attractor basin. Eventually, however, the Saturn/Mars attractor starts to trace a pattern throughout the man's life. We can assume that work will be affected in an obvious way, because both of the planets have to do with work. You know how to generate the possibilities: he might feel that he is under pressure at work, constricted in his movement and putting in lots of overtime, while on the other hand not making too much progress and probably not having much control. Responsibility without authority is a possible manifestation. Then again, Saturn in hard aspect to Mars might also affect his health, his sex drive, maybe the engine of his car. As the attractor traces out its pattern in his life it will have many different expressions in terms of specifics. Yet perhaps the most important thing is the basic underlying pattern that characterizes his life at this time, that of energy being restricted and focused. As the transit ends after Saturn's third hit to his Mars, the attractor pattern begins to fade, becoming less prominent and affecting fewer areas of his life.

While it is helpful to see how one transit could work alone, there are really multiple levels of complexity that could be taken into account. Even a single transit really implies great complexity: the transit will affect the natal chart, it will come at a particular point in the person's life, and will be dependent on choices he has made before. But practically speaking, we often have several transits and progressions of varying intensities going on at the same time. When that happens, we get pulled between the energy of one attractor and the others. From the perspective of an astrologer, we often see this as a series of isolated events indicating the various astrological happenings. From the perspective of the person in the midst of this, it usually seems like a particular time in their life. It has a distinct flavor, although that flavor may be indecision, confusion, or ambivalence.

This is perhaps most obvious at those times when the outer planets form a hard aspect in the sky, as when Saturn is opposing Uranus. Individuals may then have their natal chart hit by these planets almost simultaneously. The man in our example could be pulled towards two attractors, Saturn/Mars and Uranus/Mars at the same time. The pull of these two attractors will trace out a complex but discernible pattern in his life, although one that is not nearly as easy to describe as a single transit.

Summary

The two concepts of fractals and attractors are potentially valuable additions to the astrologer's vocabulary. As you can see, incorporating them does not require changing much astrology, per se (in fact, as long as you go along with everything I am saying in this book, you don't have to change anything!). It is more a matter of adopting a new terminology than adapting to new concepts. The fractal-like nature of astrological symbols should be readily apparent, and archetypes have much in common with attractors.

Fractals are a great way to explain the multivalent aspects of astrological symbols, carrying the same meaning in various manifestations. The concept of attractors can free us from the need for precision in knowing how astrological symbols will manifest. We don't need to know precisely what is going to happen—at any level—in order to assert that there is a meaningful coherence to astrological symbols. We can point to natural phenomena and human activities up to the level of whole societies and economies as models of how an overall pattern can be discerned without knowing the exact nature of the next occurrence. Astrologers are no more vague than meteorologists, economists, and those in many other disciplines, and the concept of an attractor gives us a model for explaining how astrology works without being rigidly precise. More than answering critics, astrologers themselves can see why they ought to have a degree of latitude in the process of interpretation. Perhaps the greatest value in using the concept of attractors is that it is an alternative model that frees us from using causal language to talk about astrology.

As evolution of consciousness proceeds, it is obvious that the nature of astrological attractors will become more complex and less certain. Preconventional and conventional astrologies necessarily have fewer options for how symbols can come into being than postconventional astrologies, and within each of those broad levels the higher substages will have more options than the lower. We also live in an increasingly complex world, with a multi-level and multi-perspectival cultural matrix that greatly enriches the possibilities inherent in any astrological symbol.

CHAPTER 10
CONSULTING

My intention in writing this book has never been to show astrologers how to consult. Instead, I have tried to suggest reasonable parameters for the process of astrological consulting, and to help astrologers to frame their discipline in a way that will be practically productive and intellectually satisfying.

I realize, however, that it might be helpful to demonstrate how an astrologer could use some of the ideas in this book in the consulting room. Assuming that you attract the right clients for your practice and have a good idea about the type of astrology you do, applying the basic concepts is not difficult.

Throughout this book I have been emphasizing that astrology does not describe the vertical dimension of development, the evolution of consciousness, it only describes the conditions that will prevail on any of those levels. That leaves the astrologer in an awkward place, however, because knowing what astrology does not take into account won't be much of a help without knowing how to fill in the blanks.

Here we run into a potential problem, because astrologers aren't really in any position to make assumptions about anyone's level of consciousness. In fact, it is a process that most psychologists wouldn't be up to, either. The evolution of consciousness is very complex, and while it helps to imagine that a person can be conventional or postconventional, or a second or third chakra person, or Blue or Orange or Green, the reality is that even within a single area of life there can be movement among adjacent levels. There is a general evolutionary trajectory, but there is much variation within that overall pattern.

It is excellent that we can introduce evolutionary concepts into our vocabulary, but when it comes to sitting down with a client we aren't going to be privy to this missing dimension of information. Many astrologers who do take a developmental perspective essentially give up and schmear their interpretations all over the spectrum, figuring the one's that are relevant will take hold in the client's psyche. Others make the mistake of thinking that astrology does contain the evolutionary information, and that it can be read from the chart.

We shouldn't underestimate the problem, because there are all kinds of undesirable effects that could result from thinking that we have zeroed in on a client's developmental level. For example, one negative consequence of a developmental perspective is that it can leave us open to condescension. "I'm postconventional," says the astrologer, "but the client is *only* a conformist at the conventional level," or, "I'm a heart chakra person but he is a third chakra person." Such condescension brings into question the astrologer's own perspective—especially since he or she may be wrong in their assessment of both the client and themselves. Condescension and failure to appreciate the value of other developmental levels is an issue until we get relatively high on the developmental ladder.

But aside from the problems associated with condescension, there is the simple question of accuracy. How could the astrologer know where the client is? The answer is that you can't really have much insight into the client's developmental perspective from what takes place in the course of an astrological reading. Remember that development is complex, and a client can be all over the spectrum, postconventional in their relationships, conventional in their career, with perhaps a dash of preconventional in their religious outlook, for example. They can also be at a transition point between developmental levels, and they may be dealing with a particularly stressful time that causes them to temporarily regress to an earlier level.

What we *can* do is listen to clients about the issues that are of concern to them. Although it isn't an assessment of their overall evolutionary growth, and while it may fall short of telling the complete story of the area of life involved, the client's discussion of the issue at hand—the issue that has brought them to you—will usually be full of clues. There are many clients who just want a general reading, and that means that you need to listen a bit more carefully, but most clients are ready to plunk down some cash because they have an issue.

I mentioned earlier that I've noticed that there are three basic questions that clients ask, although they can take many, many forms. These three questions are a good source of clues about what is of most concern to a client. The first is "what's going to happen?" This question comes with the implication that there is a knowable future, and it implies a conventional perspective. When this question is dominant, the client is asking you not only for future conditions, stresses, and opportunities, but also for an outcome ("where is this going?").

The next question is "what can I do?" This is a postconventional question, one that usually has an Orange, achievement orientation associated with it. The person is asking about the conditions that prevail and how they can be manipulated to various ends. The future is open and the client intends to have a role in creating it, and they want to know what factors they are dealing with, usually in advance of taking any action ("what's the best route to take if I want to get to____?").

The third question needs very good ears on the part of the astrologer, and it has to come in the absence of the first. It is "what is the meaning of this time?" This question is also postconventional, but with a Greenish or Yellowish tint. The person who asks this question wants to understand what is happening in such a way that they can use it to consciously further their own growth. They understand that challenging times are opportunities for development, and that times of opportunity are challenges to the status quo. Like the people who ask the previous question, they see the future as open, but the outcome they are seeking to create is not so much (or not only) in their external lives, but also in terms of changes in who they are.

Learn to listen for these questions. You can probe around a bit for them if they aren't appearing. Sometimes just asking the client what they want to know will do the trick. Don't think that you've taken the person's developmental temperature, however. All you have is a piece of information about where the client is with *this issue*, right now. That can't even be generalized to the area of life involved, because people will often regress a bit in the process of clearing up old emotional baggage. For example, someone who is basically at a postconventional point in their career life might have a Pluto transit that stirs up memories of a really bad third grade, and suddenly they have an issue that drags them temporarily back to the conventional level where they have power struggles with authority figures. Such regressions are often necessary so that we can consciously live out some pattern that is lurking below the surface, unconsciously waiting to sabotage the progress we have made. Someone who has moved to the postconventional stages of relationship might find a partner who triggers abandonment issues that go far back into their childhood, issues that need to be cleared up before they can move forward.[1]

Astrologers are in a sense aided by the fact that clients frequently are concerned about an issue that is a sticking point for them, something that represents a developmental laggard within their overall psychic system. In those areas of life where they feel a sense of control and mastery, they are less likely to be seeking out the advice of others. That is especially true at the postconventional levels, and by the time one reaches that point where self-actualization becomes the dominant motivation in life, not only does the person feel in control, they also are far more willing and able to incorporate disparate parts of themselves into their self-image. It is therefore in those areas or specific issues where people are lagging behind that they are most likely to consult an astrologer. That gives us a little edge when it comes to espying the relevant developmental level for the question being asked, but we can't generalize that information to other things.

Occasionally, you will have a regular client who through a number of consultations begins to fill in the picture, more or less. Then you can begin to get the sense that the client is postconventional in one area while more conventional in another. You might even get a sense of the overall developmental perspective, although remember that any information about the client is filtered through you and your perspective.

It is also not infrequent that clients come to an astrologer when they are on the cusp of a transition from one developmental perspective to the next. That's because issues of a certain intensity carry with them the potential, although only the potential, to make such a move.

Although I am a Western astrologer, I have a number of regular clients of Indian origin. There are many good Jyotish astrologers around, especially with the Internet linking the world, so it's not that I am a last resort. My Indian clients are quite diverse in many respects, but they also have many similarities. For example, the overwhelming majority are female, educated, established professionals, living in the northeastern United States. They are also very likely to have been born in India, but have lived in the U.S. for a long period of time. They all express a strong attachment to their culture and its values. It is important that we be clear that I am speaking of people who I know relatively well, not single-visit clients. I don't want to be accused of making stereotypical assumptions about people. From a developmental perspective, it is clear that they are trying to bridge the demands of what they describe as the very conventional ethos of Indian culture with those of the distinctly postconventional world in which they spend most of their days. Usually, there is a clear break between their attitudes towards relationship, which tend towards the conventional, and career, where they are postconventional.

There is a palpable struggle between defining oneself in terms of a culture where there is one very particular set of expectations on a woman, and a culture where possibilities are seen as almost limitless. The constant shuttling back and forth between these value systems creates an obvious stress. From the outside, it often seems to me that these women have very clearly shifted their identity towards the postconventional values that they exemplify in their careers. In any case, that is the area of life where they seem to be happiest and have their greatest sense of identity. Yet applying that same postconventional view to relationships (for example, dating someone outside of their culture) is very difficult and something they approach with trepidation.[2]

Although they will sometimes bristle at even the gentlest suggestion that they might apply the kind of value system they have in their careers to their relationships, I have to note that these clients have come to see *me*. As I said, there are plenty of Jyotish astrologers around, and it would not be difficult to find a good one whose cultural background is also Indian, yet they seek out and *regularly* consult with a Western astrologer. It seems to me that they are seeking to strengthen their postconventional values. I don't tell clients what to do, and I don't harangue them to "grow!" or anything like that, but I cannot help but present my own more or less postconventional psychological astrological perspective. At times, they make it clear that they find this unsatisfactory, as they seek more definite answers that I demur to give. In general, however, they return for further consultations, an indication that they get value from the process.

I've given this example, at risk of creating several dozen kinds of misunderstandings, because it shows how clients can seek out an astrologer when they have a conflict of value levels. This example shows some rather slow-moving conflicts that may take the better part of a lifetime to resolve, while at other times clients are at a rapid change point.

Any helping professional frequently comes to the point where it seems obvious what a client should do, but the challenge is always to hold one's tongue. Telling a client what to do has several unfortunate consequences, the most obvious being that the helping professional could be very wrong about the outcome of the suggested action. Yet even if our idea about the best course of action were right on target, we would be taking responsibility away from the client. We would be limiting their involvement in their own lives.

What we can do is to recognize that many clients will come to us with two kinds of conflict co-occurring. The first is described by the astrology: let's say a tough natal aspect and/or transit. That tells us the kind of challenge the person is facing, the areas of life involved, and to some extent the intensity of the conflict. The second kind of conflict is one of growth: the suction-like force to remain where they are versus the possibility of moving forward and upward in their consciousness development. For many, it is like being suspended between two equally strong gravitational fields, unsure of which direction they should fire their rockets. An astrologer may be able to recognize that the choices offered within the astrological picture are translating into a developmental issue for the client.

For example, a man might be concerned about whether or not he will get a promotion at work. He has put in years of solid service and has a great reputation, but for the last several years he has been passed over. Only recently has this become a real concern to him, and this is reflected in a transit of Uranus to his Saturn. With the help of astrology, we can probably fill in a number of details, and perhaps even get some intuition about whether or not he will get the promotion. If we listen a bit more closely, however, we might hear another dimension to his dilemma. He might talk about how he is very dependable and reliable, how he has a great attendance record, how his work is always done on time, and so on. We might also hear him saying that he isn't really complaining about not being promoted, because he has a steady job and knows he is valuable to the company where he is. That is, we could hear that he has a rather conventional outlook on his job. Yet we might also hear him say that he is getting tired of the routine, that he thinks he could do more, and that he would like to have a shot at doing something more exciting. If he doesn't get the promotion, he is thinking of applying for an outside sales job that would mean that a large part of his salary would be based on commissions. That could mean making either much more or much less than he does now, but that seems exciting as much as it sounds intimidating. In other words, he is thinking about taking a step into the postconventional world.

Astrologers will recognize that the pull towards something new and different in career, an excitement to try a new approach and break from routine, is very typical of a Uranus transit to Saturn. What we need to see in this example is that there is also a potential for growth, for the man to move from being a rule follower to a game player, from doing work he is given to creatively generating new possibilities for income. It need not be the case: his transit could just as well have him contemplating a move from one conventional job to another.

What an astrologer can do, with even a very little bit of insight into the client's developmental process, is to frame the situation so that the client sees that he is confronting a growth opportunity and not just a choice between two different but equivalent options. Framed in such a way, the client might be able to better understand what it is about the riskier job that is so appealing. Far from coercing him into making the leap to a higher level by pushing for him to move to the outside sales position, a range of options could open up for the client. For instance, he might see that he has been a good worker but has not taken much initiative, and that may be why he has not been promoted. He might recognize that he would better like the challenges of outside sales than the burden of a promotion to an administrative job, or vice versa. He might even decide to stay at his present job and apply his blossoming postconventional energies elsewhere.

Taking the developmental perspective into account adds complexity and richness to astrology, although once again I have to emphasize that the astrology itself will not say how the client will respond to the transit's potential. He could choose to remain where he is, although his attitude and behavior could change and he might not be quite the model employee he had been. He could make a bold jump to outside sales and thrive. He could make the move and be unhappy, especially when the energy of the transit begins to fade.

Each significant transit likely carries some potential for evolutionary growth. In fact, each significant natal aspect or symbol certainly contains the seeds of its manifestation on all developmental levels. But what the astrology indicates in potential is only the form and content on a two-dimensional plane, the third dimension is up to the individual, and it is certainly the case that even the strongest of transits to the most powerful of natal aspects do not necessarily lead to any real growth and development. Astrologers need to be able to listen to developmental potential—often expressed as a stress between conflicting value sets (developmental levels), but they also need to be aware that such a conflict will not always be present.

EPILOGUE
MORE THAN THAT

We seek to know who we are.

Humans look up to the stars, trying to decode meaning from the immense cosmos. We also look to the microscopic level of our genes, and to the functioning of our brains through dynamic imaging techniques. We want to know who we are biologically, psychologically, socially, historically, and spiritually.

Each of us is a concatenation of innumerable factors on many levels. Biologically, we are products of our genes (and epigenetics), our diets, and our living habits, as well as incidentals and accidentals. Psychologically, we are our histories, temperaments, inclinations, and we are the ever-changing stream of our thoughts, feelings, and emotions. Socially, we are all of the many roles we play, in our homes, with our friends, with various family members, in our careers, and in other situations.

We are all complex, multidimensional mosaics of these, and many more, factors. And the mosaic is not static but dynamic, each tile constantly changing in both appearance and position, and each in some way reflecting all the others, like the jewels in Indra's net.

Static definitions inevitably fall short in a dynamic world. Even the most enduring personality traits are in a sense transient.

I am reminded of the story of a Zen monk who went to his master, upset that he had such an angry personality.

"Show me this anger," the master said.

"But I am not angry now," the monk protested.

"Okay," replied the master, "then go get yourself into a situation that will anger you, then come and show me this terrible anger."

"That won't work," complained the monk, "because by the time I get back here, I will no longer be angry!"

"So," said the master, "you're not really such an angry person, after all, are you?"

All of our perceptions are made from the perches of our biology, psychology, astrology, and the rest. All of our ideas about ourselves are then placed back within the same nest.

Our identifications are located within a matrix of factors: sun sign, moon sign, ascendant, gender, ethnicity, profession, relationship status, sexual orientation, height, weight, eye color, introvert or extrovert, Purple, Blue, Green, and anything else you care to throw in.

We seek to know who we are, but can only look through the lens of ourselves. Our frontal lobes try to see the functioning of our frontal lobes, our sun signs seek to understand our sun signs. The web of factors that comprise us is both the object of our inquiry and the subject asking the question.

Our identifications have a limit, one that appears as soon as we begin to identify with some aspect of ourselves. We, as subject, want to know who we are, but as soon as we come across an answer that answer is no longer subject but object.

Thus, we are located within a complex matrix of physical, biological, psychological, social, and cosmological meaning, but the more we understand those meanings, the less they become our permanent address.

Such is the spiritual project, the evolution of consciousness. As soon as we decide we know who we are, we begin the subtle process of disengaging our identity from that image. On a practical level, you are still male or female, 5' 3" or 6' 4", born under a Leo or Capricorn sun, but slowly and inevitably, you become *more than that*.

In this book, I have argued for a number of ways that astrologers can and should expand their view of who we are as beings in the cosmos. Developmental level, cultural base, and other factors, are all important determinants of our identities that need to be acknowledged if we are going to serve our clients well. They are also important considerations if astrologers are going to understand their own discipline and relate it constructively to others.

Yet we don't want to make a larger cage for ourselves. The ultimate purpose of a multidimensional model is not to create a more elaborate system of pigeonholes, but to loosen the boundaries of our limitations, to learn to dance among a variety of perspectives. That's true whether we are talking about work with individual clients or about astrology as a field of knowledge.

An integral astrology isn't about my astrology, or yours. It is a means of helping us to understand astrology as a whole, as well as all of the diversity that exists within this ancient and expansive field. It is a framework for understanding what we do as astrologers in a way that will make it possible to build bridges among ourselves and to other disciplines.

It is perhaps a way to make connections should we find ourselves on a long train journey over barren territory, without a deck of cards.

NOTES

Introduction: The Beginnings of a More Inclusive Astrology

1. The New Paradigm sciences are those that in some way challenge the prevailing materialistic view (often called the Newtonian-Cartesian or simply Newtonian view, although it was really those who followed Newton and Descartes who championed materialism). Chaos and complexity theories; evolutionary theories like those of Ervin Laszlo; Rupert Sheldrake's morphic fields; and transpersonal psychology, would all be considered New Paradigm sciences. Wooter Haanegraaf, in his survey of New Age writings, considers these New Paradigm sciences to be part of the New Age movement. I think it is clear that they are foundational to the New Age, without necessarily carrying the emotional and spiritual charge of the movement.

2. By contrast, there have also been several noteworthy attempts to see an evolutionary paradigm within astrology itself. The idea behind most of these perspectives is that clues to evolution can be found within the system of astrology, for example in the sequence of the zodiac. While these ideas are often formulated into elegant self-contained systems, they usually fail to map very well onto contemporary developmental thought. For an excellent example, see Gerry Goddard in *ReVision,* Counterpoints in Transpersonal Theory: Toward an Astro-Logical Resolution, Winter 2005, 27(3), p. 9.

3. Stephen Arroyo made this point in *Astrology, Karma, and Transformation*, and he was building on the work of Dane Rudhyar. It is an extremely valuable insight, but it leaves open the question of how we will approach the evolution of consciousness. Arroyo, Rudhyar, and Steven Forrest have acknowledged the limitations of astrology, and have placed great emphasis on the development of consciousness. This book is largely an effort to add more precision to their formulations with the help of several developmental models.

4. For example, psychologist John Holland has six types in his system, which looks at the relationship between personality and career.

Chapter 1: Evolution

1. This isn't exactly correct. Enlightenment is a now recognized as being of many types, in part conditioned by developmental level, and the grand image of totally liberated figures, like Buddha or Christ, is tempered by those with a more everyday realization. Arjuna Ardagh's book *The Translucent Revolution* is about people having enlightenment experiences within the context of ordinary reality. Buddhist teacher Jack Kornfield has said that in a sense enlightenment is really the beginning of the process, because realization has to be incorporated at all levels of being, the body, and emotions as well as the mind. Thus it is possible that people who have attained enlightenment may find their way to an astrologer's office.

The relationship between enlightenment experiences and level of consciousness has been more fully explored by Ken Wilber and Allan Combs. The Wilber-Combs Matrix is presented in Combs' book *The Radiance of Being*. The point, for our purposes, is that whatever enlightenment experience, feeling of unity, etc., a client has or has had, they are nonetheless unlikely to match up to the Christ-Buddha-like images many of us carry.

2. Western psychological developmental systems such as Freud's were often based on clinical work with patients, where the express goal is reaching a state of functional normality. Normal, however, is not without its problems, such as the transient nature of existence (old age, sickness, and death, in the Buddhist view). Eastern psychological systems tended to take normal as a given, and work from there.

The history of the line of thinking on development is extensive and complex, but contemporary thought is often traced to Abraham Maslow establishing the hierarchy of needs, with self-actualization at (or near) the top. From that point onwards, the possibilities for development opened up, and many theorists began to conjecture about what self-actualization was all about, and if there were further levels of development. Jung's emphasis on the individuation process is right up there (or in there) with this, and he formulated his ideas earlier than Maslow. But Jung did not articulate a hierarchal system.

3. As Jenny Wade points out in *Changes of Mind*, functioning at the preconventional level gives prominence to structures very low in the central nervous system. The person's center of operation is basically in the brainstem, although higher functioning can be recruited to serve these very basic needs.

4. Just as preconventional perspectives are ruled by the brainstem, the conventional stages are associated with the limbic system, the emotional center of the brain. The capacity to learn at this stage is closely tied to emotional outcomes of our actions.

5. The ego is fully formed at this stage, but being an isolated ego in the cosmos is scary. One can espy apparently universal truths, and there is a great desire to align oneself with them. There is a sense that if only everyone and everything would do so, all would be well.

Chapter 2: Evolution, Part II

1. Stephen Jay Gould, an evolutionary biologist, was a champion of this perspective.

2. Aurobindo, *Letters on Yoga, 1*, section 9.

3. Spiral Dynamics is an extraordinarily accessible model for evolution of value systems, and one that I rely on very heavily in this book. It is based on the work of psychologist Clare Graves, and resonates very well with Jenny Wade's holonomic model of the development of consciousness. Spiral Dynamics is part psychology, part history, and part management manual, and the reader is highly recommended to it.

Spiral Dynamics is both theoretical and applied science in its approach. They clearly have corporate culture in mind a good deal of the time, although their work has applications in politics, education, and many other areas. Spiral Dynamics has an impressive history of practical use in a variety of contexts, showing that the perennial philosophy has a functional dimension as well as contemplative value.

4. The system Dane Rudhyar presented also emphasized cultural evolution, and addressed the complexities of individual development within a culture. Rudhyar referenced Sir James Jeans in *The Astrology of Personality*, but he doesn't otherwise discuss the source of his model. It is more or less in concert with the anthropology of the day. Jeans was an astronomer and also a popularizer of science. Jeans, however, believed that consciousness is primary to matter, in obvious contrast to the rigidly materialistic view that we frequently encounter among scientists. Rudhyar's system also resonates somewhat with the work of Jean Gebser.

Rudhyar's early stages, *animistic* and *vitalistic,* are described not only as relatively static worldviews, but also as historical processes that lead to transitions in those worldviews. Therefore, the stages he outlines would cover several stages is Spiral Dynamics. The animistic stage would include Beige and Purple, while the vitalistic stage would span what Beck and Cowan call "exiting Purple" all the way up to "exiting Blue." I think that more precise stages are useful (although the earlier stages are probably not too relevant for most contemporary astrological purposes), but the separation of animistic and vitalistic principles is also very helpful, as it is at the vitalistic stage that abstraction begins to take place.

5. According to Nicholas DeVore's *Encyclopedia of Astrology*, under Planetary: Ages of Man.

6. Jenny Wade, *Changes of Mind*. See the Recommended Reading section for more information.

7. This is very similar to the Chinese notion of five souls or spirits within us, only one of which, the *Hun*, or non-corporeal soul, is not attached to the body and survives death. The other four souls can be seen as reflecting different aspects of brain-based consciousness, although in the Chinese conception they are associated with other organs. The Egyptian view also included multiple souls, although these are often seen as being analogous to the Indian koshas.

8. When I read Leary's *Exopsychology* and Wilson's *Prometheus Rising*, I was also surprised at the materialist orientation of those books, especially coming from a psychonaut like Leary.

9. It would also seem to rule out all of the excellent research done on out-of-body and near-death experiences, veridical past-life memories, and a host of other metaphysical (or nonphysical) phenomena. Scofield is quick to point out that an open-minded scientist could not ignore the data from astrology if they would but look, and chides them for long ignoring data about the effect of the solar and lunar cycles, such as circadian rhythms. However, in keeping to a strictly materialist perspective, he does something very similar to the wealth of data suggesting nonmaterial explanations. That is particularly surprising given that he cites the work of Gary Schwartz and Linda Russek, who have done excellent work with psychic-mediums that would seem to clobber a materialistic perspective.

10. This is particularly a problem with his explanations for why astrology in general, and his model specifically, works. He begins with descriptions of how circadian and lunar cycles influence life on Earth, and then moves

towards speculation about how the significant relationships of the other planets to the sun and the moon can have an influence on their effect. His discussion of field effects is very interesting, and *The Biology of Transcendence* by Joseph Chilton Pearce and *Morphic Resonance* by Rupert Sheldrake are good background reading that could support Scofield's approach.

While the direct influence of the luminaries on biology can be measured, it is very speculative that the other planets' influence the sun and the moon significantly enough to modify aspects of our lives. It is even more speculative—and very unclear to me—why the planets would have the kind of symbolic meaning we associate with them. Why, for example, would an aspect from Mercury or Mars have a different *kind* of influence on the moon? Scofield acknowledges that his approach might run into problems when we consider astrology of things other than human, such as horary charts. I also think that he dismisses synchronicity rather quickly, especially considering its popularity among New Paradigm thinkers (like the physicist whose story opens this book).

11. Interestingly, in his last chapter, Scofield cites the work of Stephen C. Pepper, who outlines something like an integral approach back in the 1940s. It is here that I think Scofield runs into one of his major problems, tying the various perspectives to astrological symbols. That there might be some relationship is reasonable, but once again we will be stuck trying to figure out what is a vertical level and what is a horizontal symbol on each level, a sticky knot to untangle.

Chapter 3: Culture

1. It leads one to wonder what needs to be changed, the description or the result. That is, does one take homosexuality off the list of perversions and leave the interpretation the same, or does one assume that homosexuality *is* associated with a particular aspect configuration, but drop the term "perversion"? Either way, we can see that the core meaning of the symbol is distinct from any cultural interpretation, but that interpretation is always embedded in a cultural context.

2. Actually, the yin/yang distinction is usually associated with female/male, although using terms from another language helps to put that into soft focus. Literally, *yin* refers to the shady side of a river, while *yang* refers to banners waving in the sun.

3. In *Nonzero*, Robert Wright makes a similar distinction, between *competitive* and *cooperative* cultures. Like Eisler, he sees both of these cultural patterns existing side by side throughout history, although he is more sanguine in his view that they represent two poles that creatively drive evolution, and the association with gender is much less evident in his book.

4. The most recent rise of religion as well as its parallel in New Age spirituality coincided with the outer planets trip through Sagittarius.

5. So many problems arise because scientists take concrete religious dogma as representing spirituality. Religious fanatics tend to have high school knowledge of science, while scientists tend to have kindergarten knowledge of spirituality. The ongoing debate about evolution in the United States brilliantly reflects this mutual ignorance.

Chapter 4: Inside Out

1. Dane Rudhyar distinguished between *exoteric* and *esoteric* astrology in *The Astrology of Personality*. The reader is referred to that book for his thoughts on the matter, but we should see that both individual temperament and collective values (or reaction to them) are involved in one's attraction to a particular astrological orientation. It is an interesting historical note that through the first half of the 20th century it appears that inner-directed astrology was consider *esoteric*, or secret.

2. Whether we are talking about internal or external orientations of astrology, individual or collective systems (e.g., psychology and sociology), or almost any other dichotomy, it is a handy rule of thumb that each perspective has some validity and that the two sides in some way complement each other. Generally speaking, it is possible to see the two sides as in some ways containing the seeds of each other, like the familiar yin/yang diagram. Thus it is usually the most productive strategy to try to understand the pattern that underlies both sides, then to shuttle between perspectives as the context dictates. The problems tend to come in not because it is so intellectually demanding to see both sides, but because our temperaments often exert a strong pull towards one side or the other.

Chapter 5: Science and Astrology

1. Rupert Sheldrake talked about the negative effects of the professionalization of science in his book *Morphic Resonance*. He pointed out that throughout history many scientists, like Darwin, were amateurs, at least in the sense of not being identified with an academic institution. Institutional science, Sheldrake reminds us, is really something that came about after the Second World War, thus it is comparatively new. He argued persuasively for the democratization of science, and the participation of nonprofessionals. Among his arguments he made one point that is key for astrologers, which is that institutional science follows the money. To the extent that is true, there is little point in studying astrology because Venus and Jupiter cannot be marketed. I think a similar economic bias is at work against studying many other things, including Reiki and various forms of energy healing, herbology, and other alternative therapies.

2. It is a popular strategy for scientists to fall back on a principle known as Ockham's Razor. William of Ockham was writing back in the 14th century, and he made the point that when searching for an explanation, entities should not be multiplied beyond necessity. In general, this translates into something like, "the simplest working explanation is the best". It is possible, for example, to create a geocentric model of the solar system, but such a model involves all manner of objects spinning around helter-skelter. It is much simpler to invoke the known laws of gravitation and use a heliocentric model. We don't need to create new laws of physics, or complex trajectories—we can create a very functional model with what we already know.

Ockham's Razor is often used to slice metaphysics out of existence, and it is a favorite tool of skeptics of astrology and anything else that doesn't fit into a materialistic worldview. Basically, the argument runs that before we consider that there is a metaphysical dimension to reality, we should exhaust all the material explanations for anomalous phenomena. Before we accept the reality of astrology, for example, we should rule out coincidence, autosuggestion, and all other factors we can think of. That's fine if it is applied fairly, but it rarely is. More frequently, skeptics hold out that a material explanation *must* be available, even if they cannot identify it. For example, extrasensory perception (ESP) is attributed to chance. Ironically, when something even more threatening than ESP is demonstrated, like mediums contacting the dead, many skeptics actually fall back on ESP as a more acceptable explanation (see Emmons and Emmons, *The Mind of the Medium*).

The application of Ockham's Razor to metaphysics is generally biased from the start, with the assumption that the material world is primary to any metaphysical (or simply nonphysical) reality. But that assumption only holds true if you already have a materialistic viewpoint, and it is therefore really just a cultural bias.

3. The question of validity is all over psychology and the social sciences, and for good reasons. Unlike physical sciences, it can be very difficult to know exactly what it is that is being measured. The danger is in creating a tautology, where one gets results that support a concept that is defined by the results.

4. Jung (see *The Symbolic Life*) stressed the difference between *signs*, which stand for a particular thing, and *symbols*, which are generative and cannot be precisely defined. You can peg a sign to a particular, like a stop sign to stopping your car. But a symbol can always manifest in a new way. Venus can be many things, and as we'll see, symbols evolve so that the possibilities for Venus in the future are greater than even the infinite manifestations possible at this moment.

5. Kenneth Irving argues for this in his essay on science and astrology in the NCGR Research Journal, Number 1 (2010), where he talks about separating the *metric* from the *mantic* layer of astrology. This is a fine approach for scientific astrologers to take, as it will probably result in measurable results. But the mantic layer of astrology is just as real as the metric layer and just as potent in interpretation, though like beauty, the good life, happiness, and many other things, it may elude scientific measurement.

Then again, as both the metric and mantic layers ultimately refer to meaningful symbols, evidence may be elusive in either case. We could assert, for example, that a transit of Jupiter to Mars will always have an effect, although unless we are very creative in our measurements, that effect may not be apparent. As Rudhyar said, the statistical probabilities only refer to tendencies within a group, not in the individual. It is actually impossible to predict that a Jupiter/Mars transit will manifest in any particular way, even if we give the greatest possible latitude to our predictions. List ten million possible ways that the aspect can occur, and you have still not scratched the surface.

6. See Robert Hand's essay on scientific astrology in *Essays on Astrology* for a very good summary of the topic.

7. Note—readers get the answer now. Scientific astrology is limited by being grounded in the achievement-oriented, scientific, postconventional Orange stage of development. Therefore, it can get good results for persons who have their own operational base at that level, and quite probably also those at the conventional and perhaps some of the preconventional stages. But it will break down when trying to describe reality for people at levels higher than Orange, for whom the very assumptions about what reality is are different. That will probably be a hard pill for many people to swallow, but the evidence is there (see the books on consciousness evolution in the Suggested Readings).

Chapter 6: Fate, Free Will, Karma, and Consciousness

1. When behaviorism dominated psychology, the mind was considered a kind of imaginary byproduct that was generated by stimulus-response chains. Outside of psychology, too, the mind was thought of as more or less identical with the brain. Modern psychiatry is still pretty much on this track, and within the medical community, talk therapy has been replaced by the prescription pad. Clinical psychologists and other counselors still use talk and experiential therapies, but they are on the defensive with this, as their ongoing battles with insurance companies show. Cognitive science recognizes mind, but even there the assumption is that mind somehow arises from the brain.

There are a lot of good reasons to correlate the mind and the brain. As a speech pathologist, I saw many people that had had strokes and other lesions to their brains, and their thinking and feeling certainly changed along with the physical changes. On the other hand, research also shows that behavioral changes—like learning a new language or playing a musical instrument—will affect the physical structure of the brain. Psychiatry's assumption that pathological mental states are necessarily the result of brain changes is flawed, because even if those brain changes can be demonstrated, it is uncertain which came first, the mental or physical.

2. Let me emphasize again that it isn't the scientific method as such that is incapable of meaningful measurement of things above the physical level, but the more materialistically-oriented tools that the scientific method often uses. True, there are some things that will probably resist measurement—love, beauty, goodness, and such. But many things can be measured if you can devise the right tools. The scientific method: observation, hypothesis formulation, testing, and analysis, is not *in itself*

all that rigidly biased towards the material. That bias comes in at the testing phase, as the result of past success rather than formal constraint.

3. Both the text of this chapter and the note above might give the impression that I am strongly down on behaviorism. It's not the case. In keeping with the integral approach, I can appreciate its value when seen within a larger context. Behaviorism is an excellent *technology*. Teachers, counselors, and therapists of all kinds can benefit immensely from understanding behavioral principles, no matter what their theoretical orientation. But that's just the point: behaviorism is a technology, not a theory of mind. When behaviorism tried to explain too much, it collapsed.

4. See Ken Wilber's *Integral Spirituality*.

5. By an odd turn of events, when *mind* disappeared, people began *thinking* there is no such thing as mind. They wrote books dismissing the role of language. It's almost a kind of Zen koan aimed at creating duality rather than realizing nonduality.

6. As I said, a rock may have a kind of consciousness. We can even assert that it does, but it is the consciousness of pure matter. A fly has consciousness. A fly will react quickly (very, when a swatter is involved), showing that it is aware of stimuli. But a fly doesn't demonstrate self-reflective awareness. I'm not a fly, so I can't say for sure, but I have not seen a lot that would indicate that flies think about themselves, where they have been, where they are going, what they would like their life to be like. In fact, not all human beings show that kind of self-reflective awareness. At the early Beige level and at least partially into Purple, there is not a lot of awareness of "me" as an individual consciousness.

7. *The Cosmic Game*, by Stanislav Grof is an excellent introduction to the many ways that consciousness and matter can be related, among other topics.

8. I am making a gentle dig at a few people, but Ervin Laszlo's *The Akashic Field* is a primary example of this approach. It is a very good read, and even if—like me—you don't entirely share in Laszlo's conclusions, you will be impressed by his approach.

9. The difference between a religious conventional viewpoint and a materialistic one is *meaning*. Although you personally aren't going to have much input into your destiny in either model, with the religious

perspective you can be assured that God's ultimate plan is meaningful and good, even if you can't see it. With a materialistic perspective, it is all just meaningless, and the good, the bad and everything else just "is what it is."

10. Preconventional societies also have a kind of universal truth, but it is particular to circumstances rather than abstracted. There can be the growing power of the sun at the winter solstice, but not an abstract idea of growth and decline contained within each other, as in the Chinese concept of yin and yang. Most importantly, for conventional thinking, the law is highest—higher even than God, in some cultures—although it is often God's law.

11. This process is also at the root of a lot of psychology, where split-off parts of the self are brought to awareness and reintegrated. Freud saw the uncovering of repressed material—whether actual or imagined contents—as the key to healing. Jung placed great emphasis on integration of the shadow, the disowned parts of the personality, as a major step in the individuation process. In both approaches, that which has been rejected from conscious awareness is acknowledged and accepted, and the result is a more whole personality. Freud took a more limited view of the material that needed to be excavated, while Jung's view included not only events and thoughts from the past but ongoing unconscious dynamics. Shamanic work, such as soul retrieval, likewise centers on bringing that which was lost back into awareness.

When parts of the personality (or soul) that were lost to consciousness are brought into awareness, they begin to lose their power to influence us. It is rather like the Great and Powerful Oz revealed from behind the curtain. We are free from the fear and power that the unconscious contents had over us. As Ram Dass said, we regain all the energy we used to "hold back the spooks." No longer compelled to act unconsciously, we are in a very real sense freed from our karma. Past life regressions offer the possibility to go even further back into the roots of our unconscious and so alleviate even ancient karma.

12. Karma has a ripple effect. If you steal someone's pocketbook, it affects the way you think about the world, but of course it also affects how they think about it. And how they perceive the world will affect how the people they interact with will experience it. The victim of a theft may become more closed off and fearful, suspicious of others. In their pain, they become overly protective and perhaps keep others at a distance. Those others may then take that message, and they too become more suspicious, or cynical about human nature.

Watch how people react to crimes that they hear about on the news, and you will see this in action. One individual's isolated crime can create fear through an entire city. The root of these actions that seed difficult karma is the misperception that the person one is acting towards is in fact *other*, and through either conventional or postconventional means, that misapprehension will have to be dispelled. The Golden Rule, *Do unto others as you would have them do unto you*, has a karmic corollary: *because ultimately you are them*.

Chapter 7: Astrologies

1. Raphael Nasser's book, *Under One Sky* is the most thoughtful attempt to deal with this that I have encountered to date. Although he doesn't arrange astrologies according to developmental perspective, he constructs an integral astrology that is multiperspectival.

2. See *Chronology of the Astrology of the Middle East and the West by Period,* compiled by Robert Hand, 2nd ed., published by Arhat, and *NCGR Research Journal Volume 1*, Number 1, Summer 2010.

3. Karl Jasper's term, most accessible through Karen Armstrong's *The Great Transformation*. As is frequently emphasized, this was the time of Buddha, Lao Tzu, Confucius, Jesus, and many other leading philosophical and religious figures.

4. See Chris Brennan's insightful essay in *NCGR Research Journal, Volume 1,* Number 1. (You'll notice I used this journal as a source quite a bit for this book. Now, I'm not saying that I didn't look elsewhere, too, but it arrived just as I was writing this chapter, so I figured that it synchronistically fell to me to use it. Besides, it is excellent. Some of the best scholars of astrology, brought together in a recent volume—it's hard to beat for my purposes.)

5. *NCGR Research Journal, Volume 1,* Number 1 (again).

6. William Lilly and Abu Ma'shur both had something to say about character, among many possible examples.

7. See Keiron Le Grice in the *NCGR Research Journal, Vol 1*, Number 1 for an excellent summary of 20th century astrology.

8. As Le Grice notes, humanistic and then transpersonal psychologies also took off around this time. This is part of the emergence of the New Paradigm I talked about in the preface.

9. On the other hand, Chris Brennan, in the *NCGR Research Journal,* seems to warmly embrace the deterministic view, and appears quite happy that it should allow for precise astrological prediction.

10. Astrologers will perhaps have mixed feelings about the term *archetypal cosmologist.* There is obviously a distancing from *astrology*, per se, taking place and that could be troubling. I do understand, however, the need to approach academia in a way that differentiates serious and careful thinking from fluff, and *astrology* is unfortunately still very much associated with daily sun sign columns of the "find the love of your life" variety.

11. Keiron Le Grice (2010). Birth of a New Discipline. *Archai: The Journal of Archetypal Cosmology, 1.*

12. See Richard Tarnas' *Cosmos and Psyche* for an expansive review of mundane astrology. But don't forget to read *Mundane Astrology* by Baigent, Campion, and Harvey, too.

13. The absence of the signs of the zodiac in *Cosmos and Psyche* is hard for me to accept. I sense that Tarnas is trying to remain on the metric level by not invoking signs into his argument, but I doubt that will succeed in convincing anyone that astrology is full of measurable facts. The outer planets in signs of the zodiac make at least as solid an argument for mundane astrology as the aspect cycles do, and I would think something like Pluto through the signs over the last hundred years or so would probably have great appeal.

14. Fernandez's developmental system strongly resembles *Spiral Dynamics*, although with important differences. He uses a three-tier system, with each tier subdivided into three substages. His three major stages are *Consensus, Individuated*, and *Spiritual.* Consensus more or less encompasses everything from Beige through early Orange in Spiral Dynamics (preconventional through early postconventional), while Individuated has characteristics of Orange through Yellow, and Spiritual includes all stages above Yellow, self-actualized consciousness.

There are two minor problems with Fernandez's model. The first comes about because of his emphasis on evolution across lifetimes. This leads him to focus on the level of development that was obtained in the previous life, and he considers that one's *true* level of development. He goes on to say that someone whose true level of development is at the Individuated level might find themselves in a Consensus family, and so would *appear to be* at the Consensus level for a period of time. Developmental theorists agree, however, that within this lifetime an individual has to go through all stages of development in sequential order. That means that the individual has to go through all the Consensus substages before getting to the Individuated stage, just as s/he may have been a fine pedestrian in a past life and will be again in this one, but will still need to crawl and toddle before walking.

The second problem is related to the first, as Fernandez suggests that circumstances may result in a leap over one or more stages or substages of development. Again, developmental theorists and researchers agree that all the stages need to be experienced in sequential order. One can have transcendental, spiritual *experiences* at any level, but that is not the same thing as a true leap in developmental level. Fernandez himself seems to make this point when he says that individuals who make such leaps may very well have to go back and redo aspects of the skipped levels, and that leaps to higher levels will be colored by the lower levels. This topic was elaborated by Allan Combs and Ken Wilber, in the Wilber-Combs Matrix, where they showed how various kinds of transcendental experiences will be interpreted at the developmental level of the individual.

Despite these difficulties, Fernandez does bring up a very interesting point in his consideration of the developmental level attained in the previous life. Although many developmental theorists (including Jenny Wade) allow for at least the possibility of past lives, how they affect development in the current lifetime is not usually addressed. While individuals may have to go through all the stages, it is possible that we fast track to the level of consciousness we attained in a previous life. As much as genetics and environment, and in tandem with them, our prior level of evolutionary attainment may help to explain accelerated development within a particular lifetime.

There are a few other issues with Fernandez's model, including his emphasis on Truth (with a conspicuously capital "T") and knowledge rather than values, identity, and experience as the basis for his levels. He also focuses almost exclusively on the middle range of development, which is functional for astrologers but less compelling as an overall model of spiritual evolution. Most of these issues appear to be related to his close following of Yogananda, and may be more a matter of terminology than content. All in all, these are metaphysical issues don't significantly impact the value of his model for consulting astrologers, and his book is an excellent source for the practical application of the developmental model to astrology.

15. Meyers also sees the planets as correlating with development through the elemental levels, for example in the way we move from the moon to the sun (water to fire). I find Meyers' system interesting and think it is worth working with and developing, although it can be difficult to keep the horizontal and vertical dimensions sufficiently separated when using the same symbols. The requirement that we think of an element in one way when viewing the chart as a horizontal descriptor and another way when considering evolutionary levels is demanding, although Meyers makes a good argument for doing just that.

Meyers adds a new way of thinking about the elements and their associated signs and planets, the *charged/neutral* distinction. While we traditionally consider Fire and Air to be positive, yang (or masculine) and Water and Earth to be negative, yin (or feminine), Meyers suggests that we consider Fire and Water to be charged, while Air and Earth are neutral. Considering the elements in these pairings leads to some very interesting possibilities.

16. Of course, psychological astrology relied heavily on Carl Jung, and through him a kind of spirituality.

Chapter 8: Towards an Integral Astrology

1. In a similar way, the love issues of the second and fourth chakras are very different, as are issues of self-expression for the third and fifth chakras. In all cases, it is not only the issue or content that matters, but the approach to that content. Our approaches to love, self-expression, career, and so on are content areas (or developmental lines) that evolve with our consciousness. In that sense, we could talk about not only second and fourth chakra love, but also first, third, fifth, sixth and seventh chakra love (the same is true for self-expression, ethics, and any other area of life).

2. As Bruce Scofield said in *The Circuitry of the Self*, astrology is a kind of "extended grass-roots scientific movement" (p.23). This is, in a sense, the kind of research the Rupert Sheldrake argued for in *Morphic Resonance* (cited earlier in these notes). There are not only significant practical

problems confronting this approach (research takes time and often cash), there is also a sociopolitical dimension that needs to be taken into account: shoddy research from a university, government, or large corporation is likely to meet with greater acceptance than quality research done by individuals or fringe groups. It's not just what is said, but who says it that matters in research. Changing that attitude should be a priority among serious scientists.

3. An intelligent and educated astrologer could probably have worked through the material and come to understand a good deal of it, but that would effectively make him a modern astrologer. At an even simpler level, Mars could not have referred to auto mechanics or combustion engines in the 14th century, and the association with blacksmiths is weak in the modern world.

4. The last point is important because to some extent even the malefics were traditionally recognized as having positive roles when well dignified or aspected.

5. Of course, many financial astrologers have knowledge of both, and enriching astrological knowledge with other types of expertise is a sound idea, but it is not part of astrology per se.

Chapter 9: Fractals and Attractors

1. These arguments are very muddy as usually presented. That the behavior and perhaps even existence of subatomic particles cannot be known precisely but only as probabilities does not seem to me to imply the existence of free will. True, if outcomes cannot be determined in advance, then we don't live in a rigidly determined universe, but to the extent that behaviors are random, we do not have *free will*, we have *meaninglessness*.

2. The Church had tied its metaphysical authority to a model of the physical universe, and when the latter changed, the former was threatened. This is a good reason to avoid tying one level of reality too tightly to another. In other words, if some scientist finds a way to predict the paths of subatomic particles with precision, a lot of New Agers are going to feel they've lost their free will.

One more consideration is worth noting. Contemporary astrologers are quick to dismiss the question of geocentric versus heliocentric models of the solar system. "Of course the sun is at the center of the solar system," we say, "but astrology is about our geocentric perspective. It's about where the person is and how the planets relate to that perspective."

True and good, but we ought to consider the problems that the rise of the heliocentric model must have caused for astrologers. It's easy enough for most of us today to invoke differing perspectives to explain why astrology can remain geocentric (except for heliocentric practitioners), but it would have been very hard for an astrologer in the 16th century. That difficulty, as much as the rise of the scientific method, probably helped lead to the demise of astrology in the 18th century. Three hundred years after Copernicus, we were just learning to shift back and forth between multiple perspectives, moving from conventional to postconventional thinking, and it's doubtful many astrologers were able to keep up.

One result of the struggles of the Copernican revolution seems to be that Western astrology became very much a solar astrology. Having been knocked around by the heliocentric model, it seems that Western astrology decided to grab a tight hold on the sun, hitching its wagon to the center star of the model. Our way of acknowledging the primacy of the *physical* sun was to make it the *meaningful* center of our system.

3. The *I Ching* is great for seeing this, because its messages are so cryptic that they push you into coming up with multiple interpretations. At some point, instead of searching for the "right" interpretation, you usually recognize that all of the possibilities you've generated share the same basic pattern, and it becomes much easier to align yourself with a productive course of action.

For example, I once consulted the *I Ching* about a difficult work relationship I had. I drew the hexagram Conflict, which is described as strength without and cunning within. "Ah," I thought as I read through the hexagram and its advice, "this is describing him perfectly. He is very rigid and idealistic on the surface, but inwardly he is ruled by emotional considerations. He is so quarrelsome, because his outward principles belie an inner insecurity."

I was ready to close the book when it hit me that there was another possible interpretation. Our business itself was a model of the hexagram. We presented to the world as principled, efficient, and idealistic, while on the inside we were having all of these emotionally based issues. We were having trouble living up to the image we projected out into the world. Like the family that portrays itself as perfect to the community but quarrels endlessly at home, our inner world was very different from our outer. I realized that we needed to deal with the emotional issues and power struggles overtly, rather than trying to pretend we were something we were not. Our clients wouldn't buy the image for too much longer if we couldn't deal with the reality of how we were actually operating.

I was again about to close the book when a further interpretation became obvious: *I was also the image of this hexagram*. I was being all high-and-mighty on the outside, making it a war of principles, while inwardly I was engaging in a power struggle. I was arguing that I was right, when an important facet I had overlooked was that I wanted to win. I wasn't being honest with myself.

Now, it isn't like one of these interpretations was any more correct than the others. They all had their validity, and they all resonated with what the oracle was communicating. That is part of the fractal nature of divination, multiple interpretations on multiple levels. Understanding the basic pattern is key to seeing how to resolve an issue on any of those levels.

4. My undergraduate degree is from Columbia University, where Alma Mater is personified in a statue of a woman situated in the middle of the campus.

5. Almanacs appear to be trying to read attractor patterns rather than understanding causal factors.

Chapter 10: Consulting

1. Psychologists recognize that there are different kinds of regression. On the one hand, when faced with stress a person may regress as means of retreating from threatening issues. That is considered a neurotic defense mechanism. On the other hand, there is also "regression in service to the ego" where the person is aware of the regressive process as it takes place rather than being at the mercy of lower developmental reactions. Jung also saw potential value in regression. At the very least, we can see where we might need to take a step back to reorganize some aspect of development that was not totally integrated on our way up the evolutionary ladder. Maurice Fernandez addresses this in his book.

2. Because the conventional level is so tied into emotional response and learned history, the transition from conventional to postconventional can be extraordinarily difficult. Guilt is the usual penalty for transgressing the conventional rules, and that guilt is no less intense when the person is

trying to move towards a postconventional viewpoint. A common result is that a person can spend years intellectually assenting to postconventional values, yet living conventionally.

SUGGESTED READINGS

Astrology

This brief list is limited to the books that are most relevant to the themes I have presented in this book. Confining myself to the development of an integral astrology, I have not included representatives of the various schools of astrology.

Astrology, Karma, and Transformation. Stephen Arroyo (1992). This is perhaps Arroyo's clearest description of his approach to astrology, and the most relevant of his many books for the purposes of this book.

Astrology and the Evolution of Consciousness, Volume One. Maurice Fernandez (2010). A truly innovative approach to dealing with the development of consciousness for astrologers.

Measuring the Night. Steven Forrest and Jeffrey Wolf Green (2000). This is the basic textbook of evolutionary astrology.

Elements and Evolution. Eric Meyers (2010). One of the most explicit books dealing with development and astrology; Meyers has many interesting insights. The caveat that astrology itself does not contain a developmental system is maintained by the careful approach to the elements that Meyers maintains. His charged/neutral distinction is a very helpful addition to the astrological vocabulary.

Under One Sky. Rafael Nasser (Editor) (2004). An extraordinarily valuable contribution to astrology, the introductory interviews alone are worth the price of the book. The actual astrological interpretations are fascinating, as well. The reader can get firsthand experience of the various types of astrology, from the pens of some of the most excellent practitioners of each. Rafael is on the leading edge of the development of an integral astrology; this book is a block in the foundation, if not the entire first floor.

The Astrology of Personality. Dane Rudhyar (1936). One of the foundational texts in psychological, evolutionary, and integral astrology. Not easy reading, but very worthwhile.

The Circuitry of the Self. Bruce Scofield (2002). I covered this book extensively because I have so much respect for Scofield's intention, clarity, and astrological thinking. It is food for thought for astrologers on many levels.

Cosmos and Psyche. Richard Tarnas (2006). To date, the most comprehensive example of archetypal cosmology. The introductory material presents what I consider to be the best model of how astrology works, and the text as a whole serves as a model of how to present astrology to those outside of the field.

Astrological Practice

These books were mentioned in regard to developing an astrological practice. Any and all of them are excellent.

Practicing the Cosmic Science. Stephen Arroyo (1999).

Astrology, A Language of Life, Volume III: A Handbook for the Self-Employed Astrologer. Robert Blaschke (2002).

The Consulting Astrologer's Guidebook. Donna Cunningham (1994).

Development and Consciousness Evolution

Spiral Dynamics. Don Beck and Christopher Cowan (1996). Obviously, a book that I lean heavily on for explaining development, Spiral Dynamics is an engaging read. The chapter on the stages of change is a bit dense and not particularly helpful for astrologers, but the descriptions of the value memes and how people transition from one level to another is the best available short of more academic reading.

The Anatomy of Spirit. Carolyn Myss (1996). This groundbreaking book takes the reader through the developmental levels of the chakras, exploring the role of culture, gender, and other issues on our lives. Probably the best book available if you are inclined to use chakras as your developmental model.

Changes of Mind. Jenny Wade (1996). This book is more academic in nature and can be a challenging read in places, but it is well worth it for a truly comprehensive approach to the development of consciousness. Wade includes prenatal and after-death consciousness in her scheme, something that is rare among academic approaches. While she correlates developmental levels with neurological functioning, she also recognizes a transcendent source of consciousness that is not brain-based.

Integral Theory

The Radiance of Being. Allan Combs (2002). Probably the best single introduction to integral theory, and it includes a section on living an integral life that should be very helpful to astrologers.

Consciousness Explained Better. Allan Combs (2010). Combs explains both vertical development and horizontal expansion clearly and with many references to the arts. Very readable, concise, and entertaining.

Integral Psychology. Ken Wilber (2000). A bit tougher going, but this book will be of obvious interest to those with psychological or evolutionary approaches to astrology.

Integral Spirituality. Ken Wilber (2006). A bit easier to read, and more recent than *Integral Psychology*, but also less comprehensive. Truly interested readers should take in the pair.

New Paradigm/New Science

Global Shift: How a New Worldview Is Transforming Humanity. Edmund J. Bourne (2009). This book is perhaps the best and most readable summary of the New Paradigm. Bourne not only explains and expands the various streams of New Paradigm thought, he is clear in describing the limitations of the materialistic worldview.

The Psychology of the Future. Stanislav Grof (2000). Transpersonal psychology is the aspect of New Paradigm thinking that is most likely to grab many astrologers; this book serves as an introduction to Grof's thinking.

Science and the Akashic Field. Ervin Laszlo (2007). The ideas in this book represent an interesting sample of New Paradigm approaches to consciousness.

Indra's Net. Robin Robertson (2009). A great book. Robertson concisely relates alchemy with chaos and complexity in a readable, astrology-friendly way.

Morphic Resonance. Rupert Sheldrake (2009). Another example of New Paradigm thinking, as applied to biology. Sheldrake's morphic fields may have relevance for astrologers in a way similar to fractals and attractors.

The Evolutionary Mind. Rupert Sheldrake, Terrance McKenna, and Ralph Abraham (2005). Entertaining and provocative *trialogues* among New Paradigm pioneers.

Other Readings

The Cosmic Game. Stanislav Grof (1998). A great summary of perspectives on the cosmos.

Synchronicity: An Acausal Connecting Principle. Carl Jung (1952). Jung generally isn't easy reading, but this text, so often cited by astrologers, is an exception.

The Afterlife Experiments. Gary Schwartz and Linda Russek (2002). I include this book because it demonstrates one way of approaching metaphysics from a scientific perspective. I don't think many of the techniques used by the authors would work for astrologers, but it serves as a useful example. It also goes a long way towards substantiating the existence of nonphysical reality, and that is important for our field to understand, as well.

The Mind of the Medium. Charles Emmons and Penelope Emmons (2002). An interesting book about psychic-mediums, included because it suggests some qualitative research approaches.

The Passion of the Western Mind. Richard Tarnas (1993). A concise history of Western thinking is a valuable asset for any astrologer interested in the history of our discipline, as it sets the background of an astrological history.

www.ingramcontent.com/pod-product-compliance
Lightning Source LLC
Chambersburg PA
CBHW031257090426
42742CB00007B/497